WTON W.E.B. DUBOIS ZORA NEALE HURSTON RICHARD WRIH
MORRISON TA-NEHISI COATES JEANTOO
LORDE DEREK WALCOTT PHILIP RANDOLPH BAYARD RUSTIN MILES
OYD AIYANA STANLEY-JONES MEDGAR EVERS PAULETTE MARSHA
HOOKS JAMAICA KINCAID IBRAM X. KENDI COLSON WHITEHEAD J
NI BESSIE SMITH ROBERT JOH NSON PAUL ROBESON ARETHA FRANKLI
N TUPAC SHAKUR KENDRICK LAMAR BILLIE HOLIDAY JELLY ROLL MORT
.B. KING DIZZY GILLESPIE THELONIOUS MONK ETTA JAMES NINA SIMON
KER WYNTON MARSALIS PRINCE QUEEN LATIFAH RUN-DMC CLARE
ANCOCK GORDON PARKS BRENT STAPLES ERIC B. & RAKIM WIC
LAYNE HUNTER-GAULT JESSE JOE JIMMY WINKFIELD SATCHEL PA
IE SMITH JOHN CARLOS OWENS LOUIS JACKIE ROBINSON BILL RUSS
GIBSON JIM BROWN KAREEM ABDUL-JABBAR JOHN CRAWFORD II
AR RAY ROBINSON WILT CHAMBERLAIN HANK AARON JOHN HOP
ENRY LOUIS GATES JR. PATRICIA HILL COLLINS ALBERTA ODELL
CHARLES HAMILTON HOUSTON CORNEL WEST ROY WILKIN
RY DAMON KEITH AL SHARPTON DEVAL PATRICK ERIC HOLDER CO
NTHONY APPIAH MICHAEL ERIC DYSON EDDIE GLAUDE JR. ANITA HIL
I JR. CLAUDE CLARK KARA WALKER HERB GENTRY CHARLES FULL
VERETT JUST CHARLES RICHARD DREW GEORGE WASHINGTON CARVE
TRICKLAND COLLINS ARTHUR B.C. WALKER JR. JESSE JACKSON
ER COBB LLOYD HALL ADAM CLAYTON POWELL JR. SHIRLEY CHISHOL
YAMICHE ALCINDOR CICELY TYSON LORRAINE HANSBERRY SPIKE LE
NE ROBINSON ANNA DEAVERE SMITH CHARLES FULLER ROSA PARK
WASHINGTON MARTIN LUTHER KING JR. NELSON MANDELA DENMA
OLM X NAT TURNER MARCUS GARVEY ALVIN AILEY KRS-ONE VESE
JUDITH JAMISON JOSEPHINE BAKER MISTY COPELAND GREGORY

HAVE I EVER TOLD YOU BLACK LIVES MATTER

BY SHANI MAHIRI KING

ILLUSTRATED BY BOBBY C. MARTIN JR.

Hello,

Like all parents, I want nothing more than for my kids to believe in themselves. Every single day I hope and pray that I am contributing to their ability to believe, because that is my most important job. I have written this book in the hope that knowing about Black history and achievements will help my kids. Maybe it will help you, too.

I've wondered for a long time why Black voices are mostly missing from young people's literature, especially outside the context of slavery and the civil rights movement. This absence sends the false and disempowering message that Black history and Black achievements are not central to the American narrative. Nothing could be further from the truth.

Think of any field of endeavor and you can be sure that Black innovators have made vital contributions. The Black women and men introduced in this book are but a small handful of those innovators. They were all kids once. They all overcame obstacles because they all believed in themselves.

I hope you see yourself in these pages. I hope this book contributes to the understanding that all people—including native peoples, people of all races, people of all abilities, people of all cultural and religious beliefs, and LGBTQIA people—are central to the American narrative and the human experience.

Be brave. Be inspired. Believe in yourself.

In solidarity,

Shani M. King

Black lives matter, in America and in the world. Have I ever told you that?

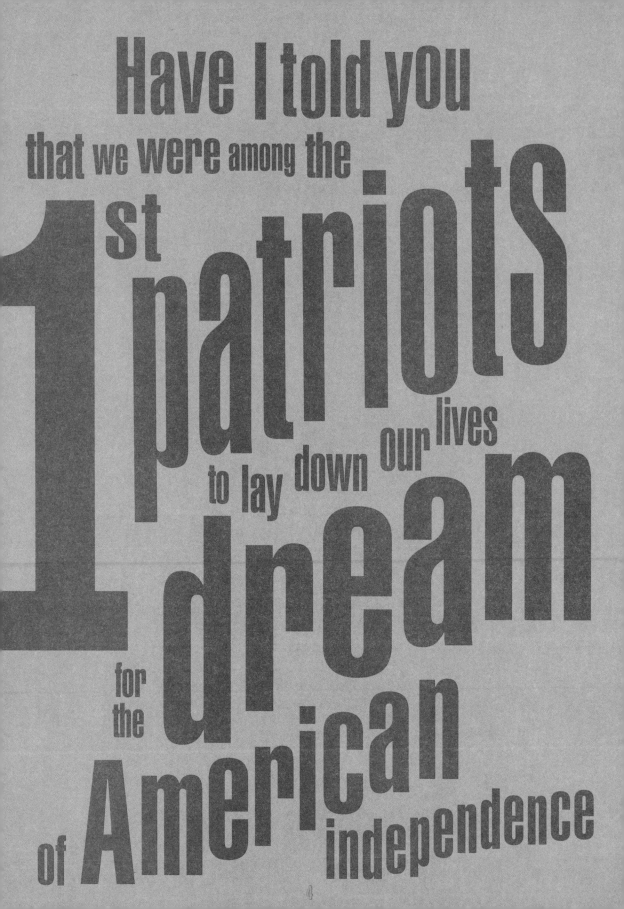

Have I told you that we were among the 1st patriots to lay down our lives for the dream of American independence

and that a **Black man** named **Crispus** was the very **first** person to **die** for that **dream**

Crispus Attucks

Have I told you that we have

never, ever

accepted that
Black lives don't matter?

not

Frederick, Harriet,

Sojourner, Martin, Rosa,

Malcolm,

or Nelson

We have always known
and you must remember that

Black lives matter.

ROSA PARKS

C.T. VIVIAN

MARTIN LUTHER KING JR.

STOKELY CARMICHAEL

NAOMI ANDERSON

BAYARD RUSTIN

CLAUDETTE COLVIN

SOJOURNER TRUTH

FREDERICK DOUGLASS

NAT TURNER

A. PHILIP RANDOLPH

MEDGAR EVERS

MALCOLM X

RALPH ABERNATHY

MARCUS GARVEY

HUEY NEWTON

NELSON MANDELA

HARRIET TUBMAN

DENMARK VESEY

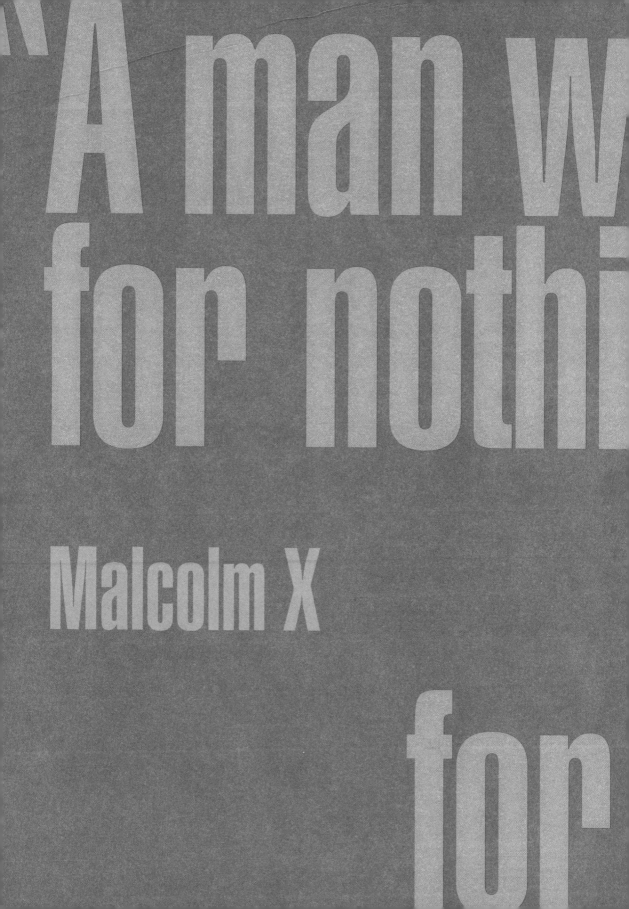

"A man w
for nothi

Malcolm X

for

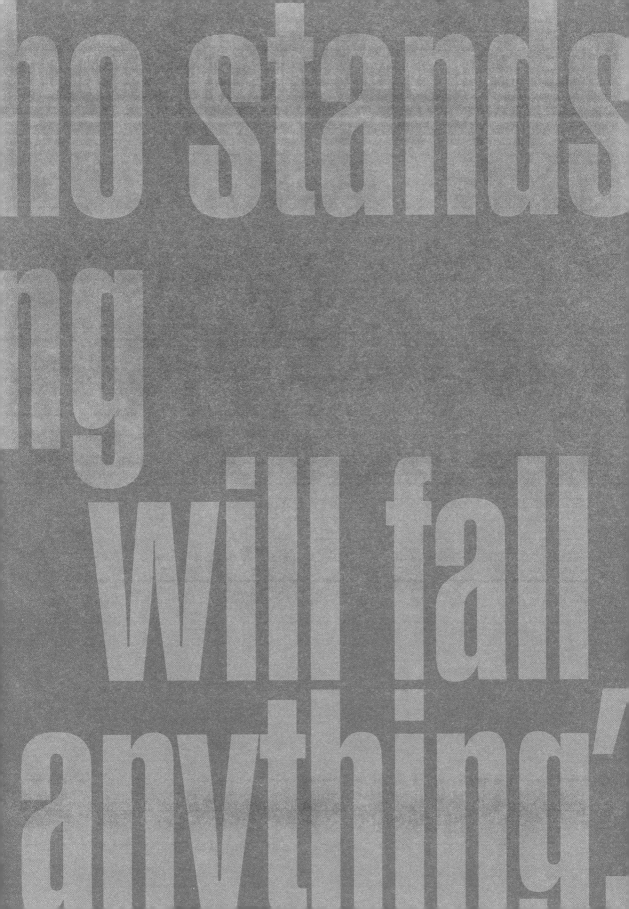

W.E.B. knew that **Black lives** matter.

"The cost of liberty is less than the price of repression."

W.E.B. Du Bois

He preached about **Black equality** and **liberation** and would be standing shoulder-to-shoulder with us today.

Have I ever told you that?

Have I told you that Zora,
we have long been Richard,
world-acclaimed Langston,
poets and James,
authors Ralph,
Maya, Toni,
Ta-Nehisi and so many others
affirming with powerful voices
that Black lives matter?

Have I ever told you that?

JEAN TOOMER

NIKKI GIOVANNI

DEREK WALCOTT

AMIRI BARAKA

ZORA NEALE HURSTON

RICHARD WRIGHT

ALEX HALEY

ALICE WALKER

OCTAVIA BUTLER

LANGSTON HUGHES

RALPH ELLISON

JACQUELINE WOODSON

PAULETTE MARSHALL

JAMES BALDWIN

GWENDOLYN BROOKS

AUDRE LORDE

DOROTHY WEST

JAMAICA KINCAID

COLSON WHITEHEAD

TONI MORRISON

TA-NEHISI COATES

PHILLIS WHEATLEY

IBRAM KENDI

MAYA ANGELOU

COUNTEE CULLEN

BELL HOOKS

"The place
in which
won't exist
until I ma

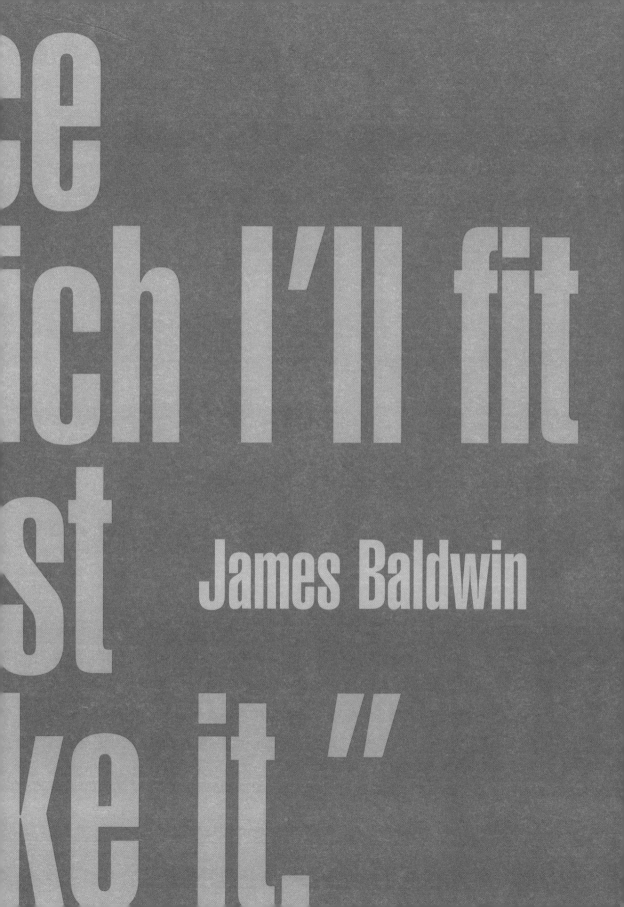

Have I told you that
we turned folk music into jazz
in New Orleans?

Have I told you how,
with trumpet notes
that floated like moonlight
on the river

Louis made the world hear that Black lives matter?

Have I ever told you that?

MARIAN
ANDERSON

ARETHA
FRANKLIN

STEVIE
WONDER

MILES
DAVIS

BESSIE
SMITH

And have I told you
that Louis marches
with his trumpet
in a long, proud history
of brilliant Black singers
and musicians?

TUPAC
SHAKUR

PAUL
ROBESON

JIMI
HENDRIX

BEYONCÉ
KNOWLES-CARTER

ROBERT
JOHNSON

I must have told you about
Marian, Bessie,
Robert, Paul,
Miles, Aretha,
Jimi, Stevie,
Tupac, and
Beyoncé,

"I don't want
no drummer.
I set the tempo."
Bessie Smith

didn't I?

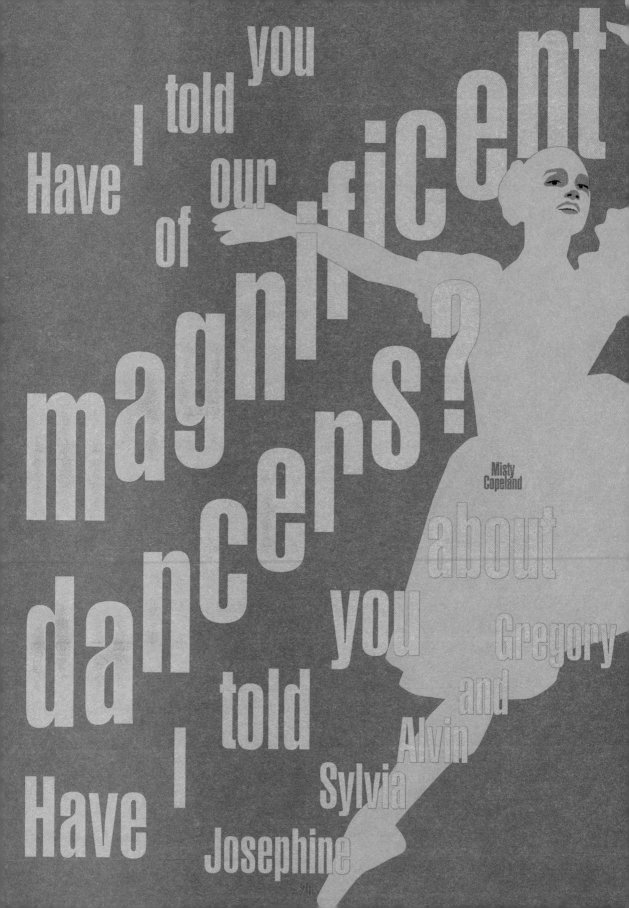

Have I told you of our magnificent dancers? Have I told you about

Misty Copeland
Gregory and Alvin Sylvia Josephine

dancing their way into history
that show
memories
leaving that
and time
for all
Black lives matter?
you that?
told
Have I ever

Have I told you
about our great
journalists

about Ida,
Gordon,
Clarence,
Gwen,
and others

their words
burning the message
on the page
that Black lives matter?

IDA B. WELLS
GORDON PARKS
CLARENCE PAGE
GWEN IFILL
YAMICHE ALCINDOR
JOY REID
EUGENE ROBINSON
CHARLAYNE
HUNTER-GAULT

We celebrate revered Black champions but have I told you about the many others who should be more famous than they are?

JESSE OWENS

COLIN KAEPERNICK

MICHAEL JORDAN

JIMMY WINKFIELD

MUHAMMAD ALI

KAREEM ABDUL JABBAR

JOHN CARLOS

JACKIE ROBINSON

Bla cham

ck
pions

JOE
LOUIS

JIM
BROWN

FLORENCE
GRIFFITH JOYNER

SERENA
WILLIAMS

SATCHEL
PAIGE

SIMONE
BILES

BILL
RUSSELL

ARTHUR
ASHE

ALTHEA
GIBSON

Maybe you've heard of
Joe, Jackie, Kareem, Muhammad,
Michael, Serena, Florence,
and Simone, but have you heard
of Jimmy, Satchel, Arthur,
and Althea too?

TOMMIE
SMITH

Do you know that Colin kneeled on a football field John and Tommie on an Olympic podium? before that, Jesse of racial superiority

Tommie Smith

forty-eight years before

to protest racial injustice,

raised   fists   for
                                justice

And   that   thirty-   years
                    two

John Carlos

punctured the Nazi myth

with four gold medals?

Have I told you that we are brilliant academics, lawyers, advocates, and judges?

THURGOOD MARSHALL

LORETTA LYNCH

ALAIN LOCKE

ERIC HOLDER

ALLISON DAVIS

SHERRILYN IFILL

MICHAEL ERIC DYSON

ROY WILKINS

ANNETTE GORDON-REED

Have you heard the courageous words of

Alberta, Roy, Charles, Cornel, Henry, Thurgood, and Sherrilyn

testifying that Black lives matter? Oh yes, Black lives matter.

ALEXAND. CRUMMELL

CORNEL WEST

AL SHARPTON

ALBERTA ODELL JONES

DEVAL PATRIC

HENRY LOUIS GATES JR.

PATRICIA HILL COLLINS

JOHN HOPE FRANKLIN

ANITA HILL

I don't have to tell you that we're creative, but have I told you about artists like Jacob and Jean-Michel and children's book illustrators like Ashley and Jerry? Let their work feed your dreams. Know that Black lives matter.

Jacob Lawrence

Jean-Michel Basquiat

Ashley Bryan　Jerry Pinkney

Kara Walker

Claude Clark

Herb Gentry

Jean-Michel Basquiat

31

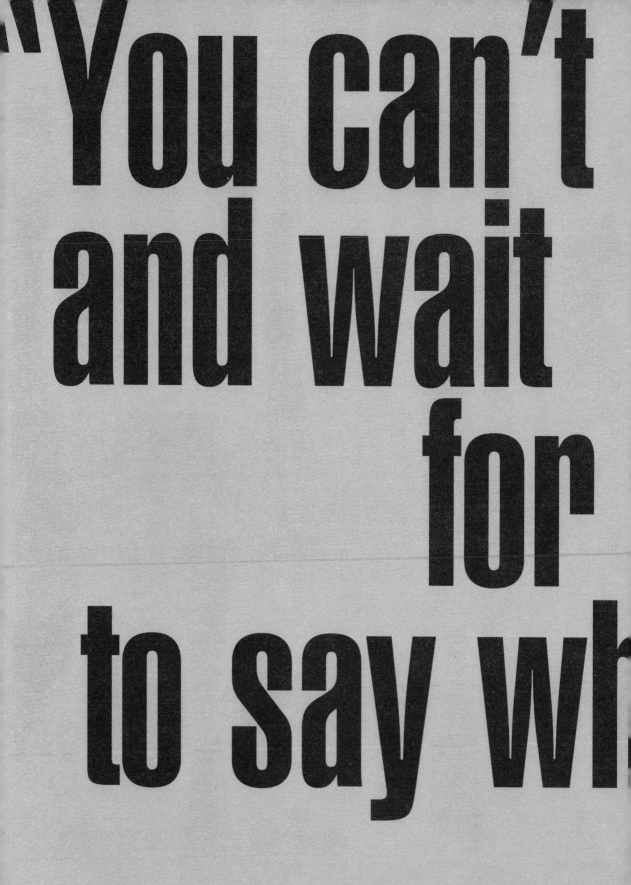

sit around.

somebody.
o you are."

Faith Ringgold

I must have told you that we are

ground-
breaking

scientists and
medical
researchers.

George, Ernest,
Charles,
I must have
told you about Marie,
Katherine, Neil
and

didn't I?

ERNEST
EVERETT
JUST

DOROTHY
JOHNSON
VAUGHAN

NEIL
DEGRASSE
TYSON

JEWEL
PLUMMER
COBB

ARTHUR
B C WALKER JR

George Washington Carver

JESSE
ERNEST
WILKINS JR

MARGARET
JAMES STRICKLAND COLLINS

Have I told you abo of brilliant actors, directors, playwri screenwriters? Ha about August, Lorr Harry, Spike, Ange and Oprah?

AUGUST WILSON

SPIKE LEE

HARRY BELAFONTE

ANGELA BASSET

OPRAH WINFREY

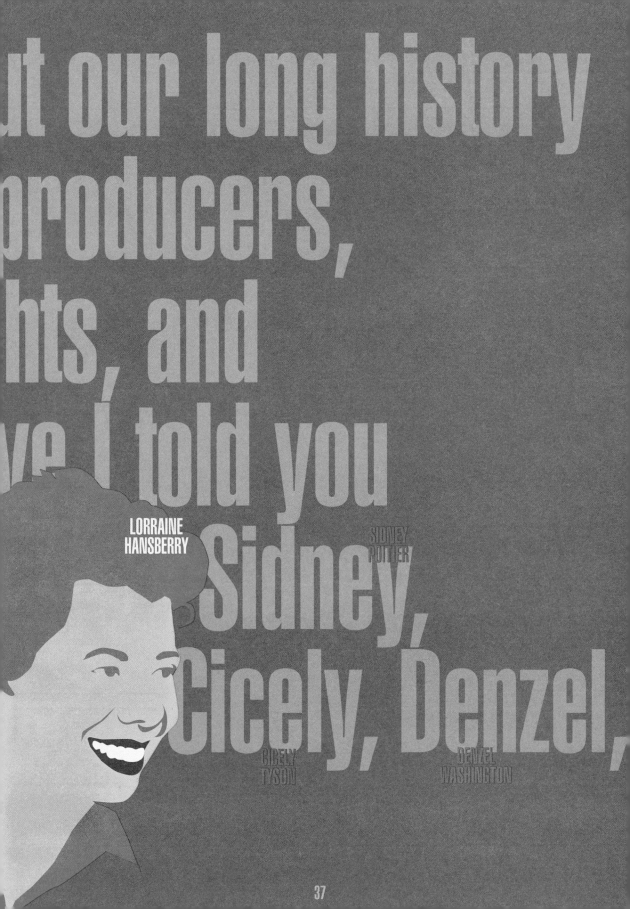

ut our long history
producers,
hts, and
ve I told you
Sidney,
Cicely, Denzel,

LORRAINE
HANSBERRY

SIDNEY
POITIER

CICELY
TYSON

DENZEL
WASHINGTON

Have I told you how our statesmen and stateswomen John, Kamala, Jesse, others Shirley, so many Adam, and to build Ayanna, worked Barack, have world? a better

John Lewis

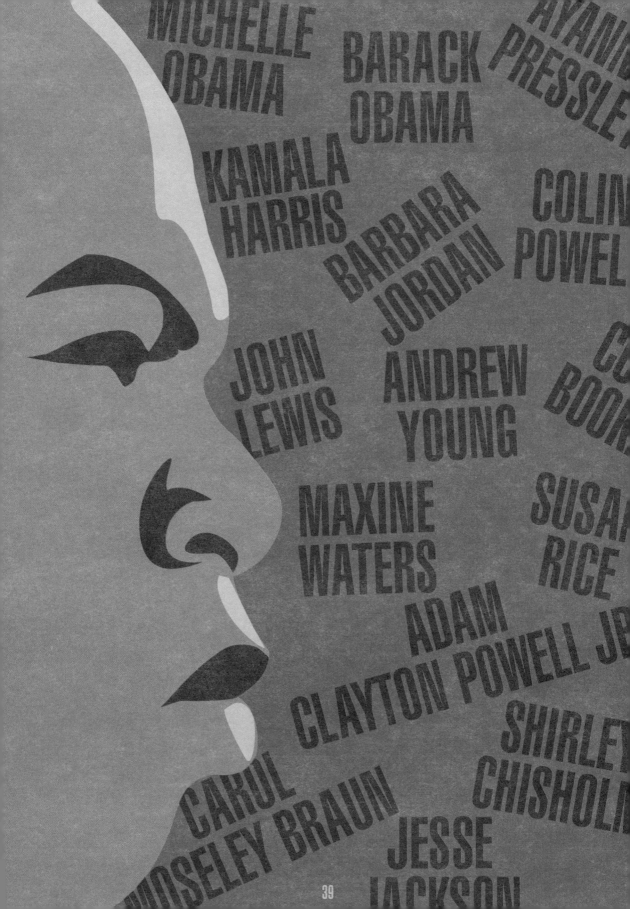

"My mother did not raise me to ask for permission to lead."

Ayanna Pressley

Have I told you that we are astronauts, exploring space?

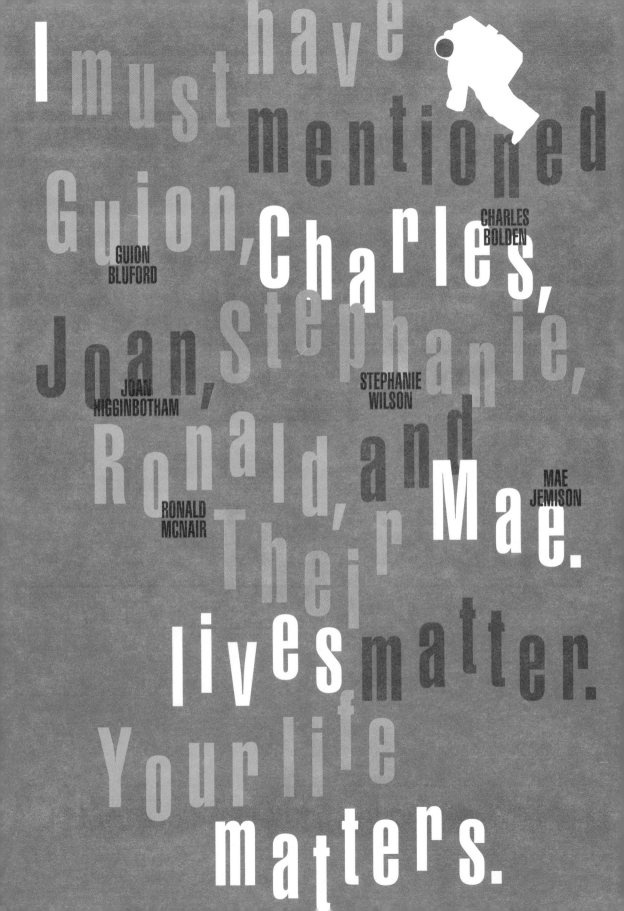

I must have mentioned Guion, Charles, Stephanie, Joan, Ronald, and Mae. Their lives matter. Your life matters.

GUION BLUFORD

CHARLES BOLDEN

STEPHANIE WILSON

JOAN HIGGINBOTHAM

RONALD MCNAIR

MAE JEMISON

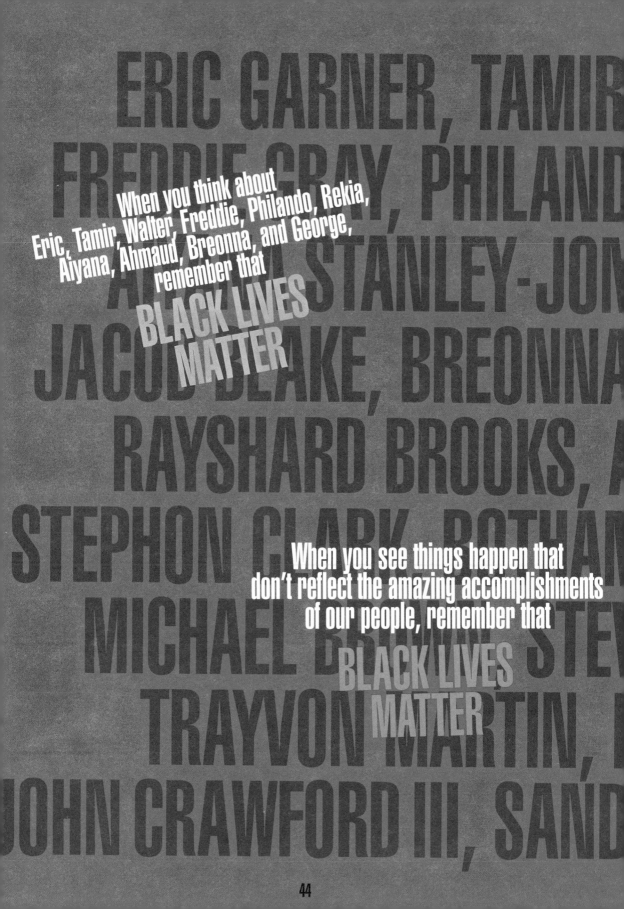

When you think about Eric, Tamir, Walter, Freddie, Philando, Rekia, Aiyana, Ahmaud, Breonna, and George, remember that BLACK LIVES MATTER

When you see things happen that don't reflect the amazing accomplishments of our people, remember that BLACK LIVES MATTER

ERIC GARNER, TAMIR FREDDIE GRAY, PHILAND STANLEY-JON JACOB BLAKE, BREONNA RAYSHARD BROOKS, A STEPHON CLARK, BOTHAM MICHAEL BROWN, STE TRAYVON MARTIN, JOHN CRAWFORD III, SAND

RICE, WALTER SCOTT, CASTILE, REKIA BOYD, ES, AHMAUD ARBERY, TAYLOR, GEORGE FLOYD, TATIANA JEFFERSON, JEAN, ALTON STERLING, EN DEMARCO TAYLOR, AQUAN MCDONALD, RA BLAND, MICHAEL DEAN

When you see things happen that don't reflect the proud history of our people, remember that

BLACK LIVES MATTER

You come from a tradition of excellence and resilience—
music that spans generations, continents, and genres; literary masterpieces that transcend
time. You stand on the shoulders of giants, my wonderful child.

I SEE YOU

YOU ARE VALUED

WE ARE VALUED

YOUR LIFE MATTERS

BLACK M

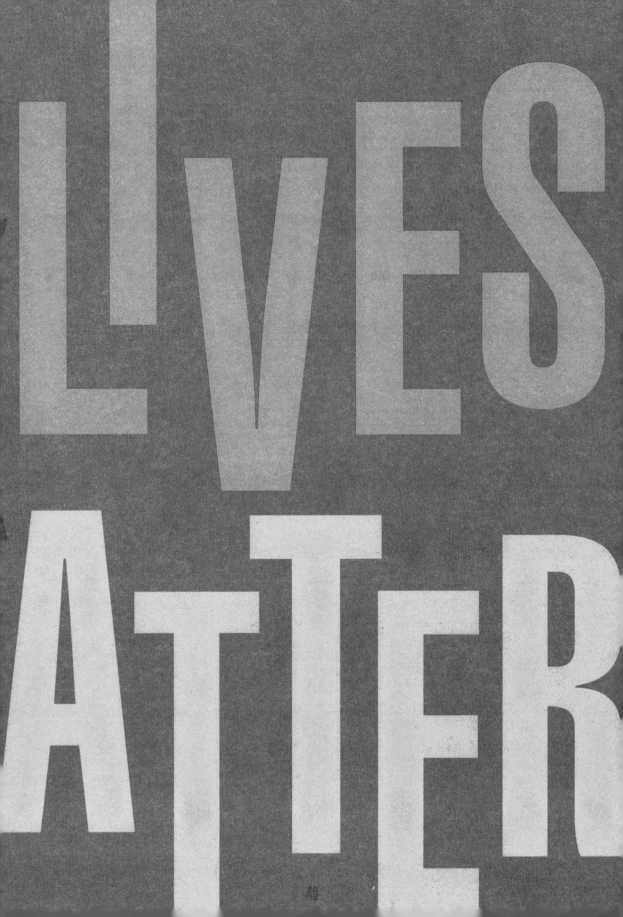

116 Lives

A brief telling of a life cannot include every character-defining event or accomplishment, and 116 such tellings are only a tiny sample of the Black lives who deserve to shine in a book like this. Music lovers might ask, why Louis Armstrong and Miles Davis but not other pioneering jazz musicians? Why Bessie Smith and Aretha Franklin but not other great female jazz and blues singers? Those are the questions I kept asking myself, over and over.

I don't mean to claim that these 116 people matter more than thousands of others I could have chosen, but there is great collective power in the breadth and richness of their contributions. They show how 116 unique arcs through history were self-created from 116 very different starting points.

I'm indebted to the scholars and friends who helped me with these life sketches, and to the writers and researchers—too many to name—who have recorded and proclaimed the accomplishments and aspirations of Black people everywhere. I hope you will take from this book the certainty that all Black lives matter—that your life matters. Your journey from where you are now can take you anywhere.

—Shani

Adam Clayton Powell Jr.
(1908–1972)

"Unless man is committed to the belief that all mankind are his brothers, then he labors in vain and hypocritically in the vineyards of equality."

As the pastor of Harlem's 10,000-member Abyssinian Baptist Church, organized a "Don't Buy Where You Can't Work" campaign that opened New York jobs to African Americans. Represented Harlem for twenty-six years in the US Congress, where he advocated for civil rights and sought to bar federal funds from segregated institutions, a provision that was incorporated into the Civil Rights Act of 1964.

Alain Leroy Locke
(1885–1954)

"Art must discover and reveal the beauty which prejudice and caricature have overlaid."

The first African American Rhodes Scholar and a writer, critic, and philosopher who thought of race as a cultural, socially constructed phenomenon. Called the "Father of the Harlem Renaissance" for his 1925 anthology *The New Negro*. Taught at Howard University beginning in 1912, chairing the Philosophy Department until 1953. Believed that the primary responsibility of a Black artist—like any artist—is to express his or her individuality. This put him at odds with W. E. B. Du Bois, who felt that Black artists should represent the Black experience.

Alberta Odell Jones
(1930–1965)

"Yeah, but I've got one strike left, and I've seen people get home runs when all they've got left is one strike."

Graduated fourth in her class from Howard University Law School and practiced law in her hometown of Louisville, Kentucky, where she negotiated the first professional fight contract of Cassius Clay (later Muhammed Ali). Civil rights activist, participating in marches in Louisville and the 1963 March on Washington. Registered 6,000 African American voters, helping to oust Louisville's mayor in a 1961 election. In 1965 became the first woman and person of color appointed city attorney of Louisville. When told she had two strikes against her as a woman and a Negro, she answered with the words above.

Alexander Crummell
(1819–1898)

"Strive to make something of yourself, then, strive to make the most of yourself."

Abolitionist leader, Episcopal priest, and major influence on W. E. B. Du Bois. Born in New York City to a free woman of color and a former slave. Spent twenty years in Liberia as an Episcopal missionary promoting Pan-Africanism, his belief that Black people around the world should unite for racial solidarity. Later founded the first independent Black Episcopal church in Washington, DC.

Allison Davis
(1902–1983)

Born William Boyd Allison Davis, a son and grandson of Black activists who became a social anthropologist. Joined the University of Chicago faculty in 1942, the first Black faculty member at a major American university. His pioneering research on the cultural and class biases of intelligence tests contributed to the discontinuance of such tests in many US cities and the founding of the federal Head Start Program. His books include *Children of Bondage* (1940), *Deep South* (1941), and *Leadership, Love, and Aggression*, a psycho-social study of the lives of four prominent black leaders and intellectuals: Frederick Douglass, W. E. B. DuBois, Richard Wright, and Martin Luther King, Jr. (1983).

Althea Gibson
(1927–2003)

"In the field of sports, you are more or less accepted for what you do rather than what you are."

Tennis player and the first Black athlete to play and win at Wimbledon (1951). Born in South Carolina to sharecroppers on a cotton farm, grew up in Harlem, where her parents moved in 1930 at the onset of the Great Depression. Quit school at age 13, lived for stretches in a shelter for abused children. Tall (5 feet 11 inches) and powerful, she won the French Open (1956), Wimbledon and US Open titles in 1957 and again in 1958, and 51 other singles and doubles championships.

Alvin Ailey
(1931–1989)

"To be who you are and become what you are capable of is the only goal worth living."

Dancer, choreographer. Born in the Texas cottonfields, abandoned by his father when he was three months old, grew up picking cotton and working as a domestic in white homes, feeling "miserable" and "very alone." Followed his mother to Los Angeles in 1942. Fell in love with dance in the late 1940s. Founded the Alvin Ailey American Dance Theater in New York City in 1958 to express the African American experience through dance. His signature choreographic work, *Revelations* (premiered at New York's 92nd Street Y in 1960), tells the African American story through dances set to spirituals, gospels, and blues.

Andrew Young
(1932–)

"Influence is like a savings account; the less you use it, the more you've got."

Pastor, US Congressman representing Georgia (1973–1977), first African American ambassador to the United Nations (1977–1979), mayor of Atlanta (1982–1990). Civil rights activist, named executive director of the Southern Christian Leadership Conference in 1964, jailed for participation in protests in St. Augustine, Florida (1964), Selma, Alabama (1965), and Atlanta (1966). Was in Memphis with Martin Luther King Jr. when King was assassinated in 1968.

Angela Bassett
(1958–)

"I'm a Black woman from America. My people were slaves in America, and even though we're free on paper and in law, I'm not going to allow you to enslave me on film."

Actress whose many movie credits include *What's Love Got to Do with It?* (1993, earning her a Golden Globe Award for Best Actress and an Academy Award nomination), *Waiting to Exhale* (1995), and *How Stella Got Her Groove Back* (1998). As her words above make clear, she is unapologetic about her preference for portraying strong, independent women.

Anna Deavere Smith
(1950–)

"My work is about giving voice to the unheard and reiterating the voice of the heard in such a way that you question or reexamine what is the truth."

Playwright and actor with numerous film and TV credits. She wrote the award-winning one-woman documentary plays *Fires in the Mirror* (1992) and *Twilight: Los Angeles, 1992* (1993), performing multiple diverse roles based on her interviews of participants in the Crown Heights (Brooklyn) and Los Angeles riots of 1991 and 1992, respectively.

Annette Gordon-Reed
(1958–)

"History is not just about the things we like or the people we want to love and admire."

Historian and law professor whose honors include the Pulitzer Prize in History (2009) and the National Book Award (2008) for *The Hemingses of Monticello: An American Family*. Her books also include *Race on Trial: Law and Justice in American History* (2002).

Aretha Franklin
"the Queen of Soul"
(1942–2018)

"Music is universal—universal and transporting."

Winner of eighteen Grammy Awards and the first woman inducted into the Rock and Roll Hall of Fame. Aretha Louise Franklin was born in Memphis but grew up in Detroit, where her father, C. L. Franklin, was pastor of the New Bethel Baptist Church. Her mother, who moved to Buffalo after separating from Aretha's father

in 1948, died when Aretha was nine. Aretha's grandmother and others, including gospel singer Mahalia Jackson, helped care for Aretha and her siblings. Aretha began soloing in her father's church at age 10 and joined his nationwide "gospel caravan" preaching tours by age 12. She began recording in 1960, and her hit songs grew to include "Respect," "I Say a Little Prayer," "Chain of Fools," and 109 other charted singles. She sold more than 75 million records and was named by *Rolling Stone* magazine the greatest singer of all time.

Arthur Robert Ashe Jr.
(1943–1993)

"Every time you win, it diminishes the fear a little bit. You never really cancel the fear of losing; you keep challenging it."

A tennis player, the first Black player selected to the US Davis Cup team, and author of the three-volume book *A Hard Road to Glory: A History of the African-American Athlete* (1988) and the memoir *Days of Grace*, which he finished less than a week before his death. An activist and spokesperson against racial injustice, arrested twice while demonstrating in Washington, DC. Winner of the US Open (1968) and Wimbledon (1975), attaining world #1 rankings in both years. Learned tennis on Richmond, Virginia's largest Blacks-only public playground, where his father was the caretaker.

Arthur Mitchell
(1934–2018)

"I bucked society, and an art form that was three, four hundred years old, and brought Black people into it."

Ballet dancer who was, in 1955, the first African American to dance with the New York City Ballet. Born into a poor family in Harlem, he became his family's principal breadwinner at the age of 12 when his father was incarcerated. He worked a variety of jobs, also becoming involved with gang life for a time. Encouraged by a junior high school guidance counselor, he was accepted to the highly selective High School for the Performing Arts in New York and began training in classical ballet. New York City Ballet director George Balanchine mentored Mitchell and created dance roles for him. Mitchell later appeared in Broadway shows and founded the National Ballet Company of Brazil, returning to New York after the assassination of Martin Luther King Jr. to found the Dance Theatre of Harlem and nurture the talents and careers of young Black dancers.

Ashley Bryan
(1923–)

"I never gave up. Many were more gifted than I, but they gave up. They dropped out. What they faced out there in the world—they gave up."

Award-winning writer and children's book illustrator. Born in Harlem, he grew up with six siblings in a home in the Bronx filled with art and music. His studies at the Cooper Union Art School were interrupted by World War II. He landed at Omaha Beach on D-Day as part of a segregated Army battalion, and later studied philosophy in an effort to understand war. He was a college art professor until 1988 and became, in 1962, the first African American to write and illustrate a published children's book. His many children's books, mostly about the African American experience, are beloved by readers of all ethnicities.

"Think about how many great works of art or game-changing ideas were ahead of their time—their creator's talent underappreciated until many years later. That's how we need to treat our young people— because who knows where the next great idea will come from?"

August Wilson
(1945–2005)

"Have a belief in yourself that is bigger than anyone's disbelief."

Playwright and two-time winner of the Pulitzer Prize for Drama. He was the fourth of six children born in Pittsburgh to Frederick August Kittel Sr., a German immigrant, and Daisy Wilson, an African American from North Carolina who cleaned homes for a living, raised her children alone, and whose last name he later took. Biracial, he struggled to

find a sense of identity. He dropped out of three high schools, worked menial jobs, and educated himself by reading in the Carnegie Library of Pittsburgh. His *Pittsburgh Cycle* of ten plays, each covering a decade of twentieth-century African American life, earned a Tony Award, two Pulitzers, and four New York Drama Critics' Circle Awards.

Ayanna Pressley
(1974–)

"Let me be abundantly clear: I am Black, and I am a woman, and I embrace both of those facts."

Politician and Massachusetts' first Black Congresswoman. Raised in Chicago by her mother, she attended Boston University from 1992 to 1994 but dropped out to work full-time when her mother lost her job. She worked on the staffs of US Representative Joseph P. Kennedy II and US Senator John Kerry and was elected to the Boston City Council in 2009, the first woman of color to serve in the council's 100-year history. She won four additional terms on the council and was elected to the US House of Representatives in 2018.

Barack Hussein Obama
(1961–)

"Change will not come if we wait for some other person or if we wait for some other time."

First Black president of the United States, elected 2008, reelected 2012. US Senator from Illinois, 2005–2008. Won the Nobel Peace Prize in 2009. Enacted the Affordable Care Act in 2010 despite bitter Republican opposition, delivering insurance coverage to at least 20 million previously uninsured Americans. Born in Honolulu to a white mother from Kansas and a Black father from Kenya who met while students at the University of Hawaii but divorced in 1964. Barack's father returned to Kenya to become a senior government economist, visiting his son only once in Hawaii (Christmas 1971) before dying in a 1982 automobile accident. Barack's mother married an Indonesian fellow graduate student, and Barack lived in Indonesia from 1967 to 1971, when he returned to Hawaii to live with his maternal grandparents. Barack struggled at times with his biracial heritage but came to see it as a strength, describing his extended family as a mini–United Nations. Attended Occidental College in Los Angeles, graduating from Columbia University in 1983 and Harvard Law School in 1991. Community organizer on Chicago's South Side, 1985–1988. Published his memoir *Dreams from My Father* in 1995. Taught constitutional law at the University of Chicago Law School, 1992–2004.

"The opportunity that Hawaii offered—to experience a variety of cultures in a climate of mutual respect— became an integral part of my world view and a basis for the values that I hold most dear."

Bessie Smith
"Empress of the Blues"
(1894–1937)

"I ain't good-lookin', but I'm somebody's angel child."

Her father died when she was a baby, her mother when she was nine, after which she was raised in poverty by an older sister and sang for spare change on the streets of Chattanooga with a brother playing guitar. Possessor of a powerful contralto voice, she met and was mentored by Ma Rainey, the "Mother of the Blues," began recording for Columbia Records in 1923, and became the top attraction in the Black-owned Theater Owners Booking Association, traveling between gigs in a custom-built railroad car. Her lyrics stressed fearlessness, sexual freedom, and women's rights. Her songs included "Jailhouse Blues," "Gin House Blues," "Alexander's Ragtime Band," "Nobody Knows You When You're Down and Out," and others. Her career derailed by the Great Depression, she died in a 1937 car crash between Memphis and Clarksdale, Mississippi, and was mourned by thousands, but her grave in Sharon Hill, Pennsylvania, was left unmarked by her estranged husband until 1970, when a stone was erected by blues singer Janis Joplin.

"It's a long old road, but I know I'm gonna find the end."

Beyoncé
"Queen Bey"
(1981–)

"Your self-worth is determined by you. You don't have to depend on someone telling you who you are."

Multi-platinum, multi-Grammy Award–winning singer, dancer, songwriter, actress, and one of the best-selling musical artists of all time, Beyoncé Giselle Knowles-Carter was born in Houston to a Creole mother and an African American father in a middle-class home. Inspired by seeing Michael Jackson in concert when she was five, she demonstrated her singing talent early and was enrolled in a music-magnet elementary school and a performing-arts high school. As a member of Girl's Tyme, she competed in the national TV talent show *Star Search* in 1993. In 1995 Beyoncé's father quit his job to manage the group, which won a recording contract with Columbia Records in 1997 and changed their name to Destiny's Child. They became one of the best-selling girl groups of all time, while turmoil in 2000 led to two years of sometimes debilitating depression for Beyoncé. She began her solo career in 2003 with the album *Dangerously in*

Love, which earned five Grammy Awards and includes the number-one songs "Crazy in Love" (featuring Jay-Z, whom she married in 2008) and "Baby Boy." Following hits include "Halo," "Irreplaceable," and many others.

Bill Russell
(1934–)

"Concentration and mental toughness are the margins of victory."

Professional basketball player who led the Boston Celtics to eleven championships in thirteen seasons (1957–1969), the last two as coach as well as player. He was the first Black head coach of a major US professional sports team. Inducted into the Basketball Hall of Fame in 1969. A dominant center who elevated defense to an artform, he is one of two players in NBA history (with Wilt Chamberlain, his longtime rival and sometime friend) to gather more than 50 rebounds in a game. Born William Felton Russell in the Jim Crow South in Monroe, Louisiana, he was eight when the family moved to Oakland, California, living in poverty in the housing projects. His mother died when he was 12. Intensely competitive throughout his career, he regularly vomited in the locker room before big games; his Celtics teammates came to view it as a positive sign. Proud, private, sensitive to racism, he maintained a testy attitude toward the Boston sports

media and fans. His former teammate Tommy Heinsohn said in 2000, "Look, all I know is the guy... came to Boston and won 11 championships in 13 years, and they named a bleeping tunnel after Ted Williams." The FBI once maintained a file on him in which he was described as "an arrogant Negro who won't sign autographs for white children." He stood in the front row for Martin Luther King Jr.'s "I Have a Dream" speech on the National Mall in 1963 and ranks civil rights activism as his most important work. He received the Presidential Medal of Freedom from Barack Obama in 2011.

Brent Staples
(1951–)

"Readers are hungry for historically grounded explanation."

Journalist, author, and Pulitzer Prize–winning editorial writer for the *New York Times*. Born in Chester, Pennsylvania into a family of modest means, the eldest son of nine children. A mediocre high school student, he was not expected to go to college but ultimately earned a PhD in Psychology from the University of Chicago. His much-reprinted essays and editorials have documented how the women's suffrage movement ignored racism, how newspapers were complicit in Southern lynchings, and how slavery persisted in other forms after its legal end. His books

include the memoir *Parallel Time: Growing Up in Black and White* (1995).

"I despise the expression ['black experience']. There is no such thing. Black people's lives in this country are too varied to be reduced to a single term."

Chadwick Boseman
(1976–2020)

"I certainly wouldn't be here if it were not for those men that I portrayed, because of what they did in their lives, and the door that it opened for me."

Actor whose movie credits include a string of portrayals of Black icons: Jackie Robinson in *42* (2013), James Brown in *Get on Up* (2014), Thurgood Marshall in *Marshall* (2017), and the fictional superhero T'Challa, King of Wakanda and hero of *Black Panther* (2018), the first superhero movie to be nominated for a best-picture Oscar, the first blockbuster superhero movie led by a Black cast, and one of the highest-grossing films of all time. An only child born in Anderson, South Carolina, Boseman received a BFA in directing from Howard University, studied acting at Oxford University, and taught acting at the Schomburg Center for Research in Black Culture in Harlem. He died an international superstar at the age of 43 after a private four-year battle with colon cancer. His final film was *Ma Rainey's Black*

Bottom, based on the August Wilson play.

"To be young, gifted and Black. We know what it's like to be told that there's not a screen for you to be featured on."

Charlayne Hunter-Gault
(1942–)

"If people are informed, they will do the right thing. It is when they are not informed that they become hostages to prejudice."

Journalist and pioneer integrationist. Graduated third in her class from Atlanta's Henry McNeal Turner High School but was denied admission to the segregated University of Georgia. She enrolled at Wayne State University in Detroit, but the court case Holmes v. Danner won her the right (with help from Constance Baker Motley and the NAACP Legal Defense Fund) to transfer to the University of Georgia in January 1961, the first African American woman to enroll there; she received a degree in journalism in 1963. Shortly before graduation, Hunter married classmate Walter Stovall, who was white, despite the objections of both students' parents. Georgia's governor and attorney general publicly excoriated the marriage and threatened to prosecute under Georgia's laws against interracial marriage. Hunter and Stovall had a daughter in 1963, divorced in 1972, and Hunter subsequently married Black businessman Ronald Gault. She has held posts with the *New York Times*, PBS's *MacNeil/Lehrer Report*, NPR, and CNN, earning two Emmys, a Peabody, and numerous other awards. Her memoir *In My Place* (1992) recounts her experiences at the University of Georgia.

Charles F. Bolden Jr.
(1946–)

"I just cannot bring my little pea brain to believe that God would pick one planet of one of millions of suns and say that's the only place in the vast universe that I'm going to put any kind of life. And so the problem is I haven't been far enough away."

The son of two teachers in Columbia, South Carolina, he was at first denied admission to the United States Naval Academy by the South Carolina Congressional delegation because he was Black, but this position was overridden after Bolden wrote a letter to President Lyndon Johnson. He graduated from Annapolis in 1968 as president of his class and became a pilot in the United States Marine Corps, flying more than 100 sorties in the Vietnam War. He trained as a test pilot and was selected as an astronaut candidate in 1980, making four space flights, two of which he commanded, including the first joint US/Russian Space Shuttle Mission. He returned to the Marine Corps in 1994, serving in Operation Desert Thunder in Kuwait and attaining the rank of major general by his retirement in 2004. In 2009, President Obama appointed him the administrator of NASA, the first African American to hold this position, from which he resigned in 2017.

Charles Hamilton Houston
(1895–1950)

"I made up my mind that if I got through this war, I would study law and use my time fighting for men who could not strike back."

Grandson of a former slave, son of a lawyer and a hairdresser in a middle-class Washington, DC home, Houston was the first chief counsel for the National Association for the Advancement of Colored People (NAACP) and key architect of the legal fight against segregation in the United States. He played a role in nearly every significant civil rights case that came before the Supreme Court between 1930 and Brown v. Board of Education in 1954, which prohibited segregation in public schools, a victory achieved four years after his death of a heart attack. "The Man Who Killed Jim Crow," as he is sometimes called, was valedictorian of the class of 1915 at Amherst College, the first African American editor of the *Harvard Law Review*, and a professor of law, vice-dean, and dean of the Howard University School of Law, where he mentored nearly one-quarter of the Black lawyers in the US at the time, including future Supreme Court Justice Thurgood Marshall. He served in the Army as a first lieutenant during World War I and was disgusted by segregation in the military, as his words above make clear.

"A social engineer [is] a highly skilled, perceptive, sensitive lawyer who [understands] the Constitution of the United States and [knows] how to explore its uses."

Charles Richard Drew
(1904–1950)

"Excellence of performance will transcend artificial barriers created by man."

Renowned surgeon, scientist, professor of medicine, and the first African American examiner for the American Board of Surgery, Drew discovered methods for long-term blood plasma storage and started the American Red Cross blood bank program. The son of a carpet layer and a teacher, he attended Amherst College on an athletic scholarship and graduated second in his class from the medical school at McGill University. After being appointed to direct the blood bank effort for Britain and the United States during World War II, Drew resigned when the military insisted on segregating the blood of African Americans.

Subsequently he taught and continued his research at Howard University and Freedman's Hospital in Washington, DC. He died in an automobile accident.

Cicely Tyson
(1933–)

"Challenges make you discover things about yourself that you never really knew."

Television, movie, and stage actress known for her portrayals of strong African American women and for only accepting roles that present a positive image of people of color. Tyson's television and movie credits include *The Autobiography of Miss Jane Pittman* (1974) and *Roots* (1977), and she has won awards for her stage performances on and off Broadway, including a Tony Award for her role in the Broadway play *The Trip to Bountiful* (2013). Born in Harlem, the daughter of West Indian immigrants (her mother a domestic worker and her father a carpenter and painter), Tyson began her career as a fashion model and was the first African American to star in a television drama, the series *East Side/West Side* (1963–1964). In addition to her Tony, she has received three Primetime Emmy Awards, four Black Reel Awards, one Screen Actors Guild Award, an honorary Academy Award, and a Peabody Award.

Clarence Page
(1947–)

"Privilege is least apparent to those who have it."

Pulitzer Prize–winning journalist, syndicated columnist, and senior member of *The Chicago Tribune*'s editorial board. Born in Dayton, Ohio, he was features editor of his high school newspaper, earned a journalism degree from Ohio University in 1969, and worked at *The Chicago Tribune* for six months before being drafted by the US Army. After his stint as an Army journalist, he returned to the *Tribune* in 1971, where he remains. He has written repeatedly about African American identity; in his book *Showing My Color: Impolite Essays on Race and Identity* (1996), he argues against the concept of color blindness and in favor of embracing one's ethnic heritage. A frequent national radio and TV commentator, Page has achieved his success despite his long-undiagnosed attention deficit disorder.

Colin Kaepernick
(1987–)

"Believe in something. Even if it means sacrificing everything."

Professional football quarterback who famously protested police brutality and racial injustice by kneeling during the singing of the national anthem throughout the 2016 NFL season, a silent act of civil disobedience that inspired hundreds of professional and amateur athletes worldwide. Born in Milwaukee, Wisconsin, to 19-year-old Heidi Russo, he was adopted by Rick and Teresa Kaepernick at five weeks of age. Reared primarily in California, Kaepernick was a successful three-sport athlete and a straight-A student in high school and had a record-breaking career at the University of Nevada while maintaining a 4.0 grade-point average. Drafted in the second round by the San Francisco 49ers in 2011, he led the team to the Super Bowl in 2012 and the NFC Championship Game in 2013. His activism may have effectively ended his NFL career; a free agent after the 2016 season, he has received no NFL job offers. He said of his 2016 kneeling,

"I am not going to stand up to show pride in a flag for a country that oppresses Black people and people of color. To me, this is bigger than football and it would be selfish on my part to look the other way."

Constance Baker Motley
(1921–2005)

"I rejected the notion that my race or sex could bar my success in life."

Lawyer, civil rights activist, New York state senator, and the first African American appointed to the federal judiciary. The ninth of twelve children of Caribbean immigrants, she grew up in Connecticut, where her mother was a domestic worker and a founder of the New Haven NAACP and her father was a chef at Yale University. Graduating with honors in 1939 from New Haven's Hillhouse High School, she dreamed of becoming a lawyer but could not afford college until a local businessman who heard her speak at a community event offered to pay for her higher education, thus demonstrating for her the life-changing power of a single individual. She began at Fisk University in Nashville but graduated from New York University and, in 1946, from Columbia Law School. While still in law school she was hired by future Supreme Court Justice Thurgood Marshall to work with the NAACP Legal Defense Fund, where she remained until 1965, serving as lead attorney in many significant civil rights cases. She represented Martin Luther King Jr. (visiting both him and Medgar Evers in Southern jails), defended the Freedom Riders, authored the original complaint in Brown v. Board of Education, and guided James Meredith's attempt to integrate the University of Mississippi in Meredith v. Fair. She was the first African American to sit in the New York State Senate, the first woman to serve as Manhattan Borough President, the NAACP Legal Defense

Fund's first female attorney, and the first woman to argue a case before the Supreme Court. She argued ten cases before the Supreme Court, winning nine of them, and assisted in nearly 60 high-court cases. She titled her 1998 autobiography *Equal Justice Under Law.*

"When I was 15, I decided I wanted to be a lawyer. No one thought this was a good idea."

Cornel West
(1953–)

"Justice is what love looks like in public."

Philosopher, activist, and provocative social commentator. He grew up in Sacramento, where his mother was a teacher and school principal and his father a general contractor for the Department of Defense. He graduated magna cum laude from Harvard in three years, received his masters and doctorate degrees from Princeton (the first African American to earn a PhD in philosophy there), and has been a professor at Harvard, Princeton, New York City's Union Theological Seminary, the University of Paris, and Yale University's Divinity School. He has written 20 books, edited 13, and may be best known for his books *Race Matters* (1994), *Democracy Matters* (2004), and his memoir *Brother West: Living and Loving Out Loud* (2009). West is a frequent guest on television and radio; has appeared in movies and more than 25 documentaries; and has produced three spoken-word albums including *Never Forget*, in which he collaborated with Prince, Jill Scott, Andre 3000, Talib Kweli, KRS-One, and Gerald Levert.

Crispus Attucks
(1723?–1770)

"Don't be afraid."

Born in Framingham, Massachusetts, he is considered the first casualty of the American Revolution. Attucks was of African and Native American descent (historians differ on his heritage), possibly an escaped slave. He had spent much of his life on trading ships and whaling vessels sailing in and out of Boston Harbor. In the fall of 1768, when British taxes and regulations led to increasing tensions with the colonies, England sent soldiers to Boston. Colonial seamen like Attucks were especially angry with England, as they faced the direct threat of being forced into the British Navy. A confrontation between British soldiers and colonists on March 5, 1770, resulted in death for Attucks (shot twice in the chest) and four other colonists; six were wounded. In his subsequent courtroom defense of the British soldiers, Boston lawyer John Adams (a future US president) argued that they feared for their lives; he singled out Attucks for having "undertaken to be the hero of the night," for encouraging a conflict by his "mad behavior," and for being a "stout mulatto fellow, whose very looks was enough to terrify any person." (Attucks was said to stand 6 feet 2 inches, about half a foot taller than the average man of the time.) The soldiers were acquitted of murder, though two were convicted of the lesser crime of manslaughter. Samuel Adams (a cousin of John) arranged for Attucks's casket to lie in state for three days; more than half of Boston's inhabitants are said to have joined the funeral procession for Attucks and the other victims.

Denzel Washington
(1954–)

"Do what you have to do, to do what you want to do."

Critically acclaimed stage and screen actor with more than 50 major film credits. His first film was *Carbon Copy* (1981); his big break was the TV series *St. Elsewhere* (1982–1988). His many honors include Academy and Golden Globe Best Supporting Actor awards for *Glory* (1990), a Golden Globe Best Actor Award for *The Hurricane* (2000), an Academy Best Actor Award for *Training Day* (making him the first Black actor since Sidney Poitier, in 1963, to win the award), and a 2010 Tony Best Leading Actor Award for the August Wilson play *Fences*. Other film roles include Black activist Steve Biko in *Cry Freedom* (1987) and the title role in *Malcolm X* (1992). The son of an ordained Pentecostal minister, he is a devout Christian who once speculated that his true calling might be preaching, not acting.

DeWayne Wickham
(1946–)

"When you lose your parents at such a young age as I did, everything seems vulnerable. I was always afraid that what I had would disappear."

Founding member of the National Association of Black Journalists, editor of *Thinking Black: Some of the Nation's Best Black Columnists Speak Their Minds* (1996). As described in his memoir *Woodholme: A Black Man's Story of Growing Up Alone* (1995), he was orphaned at the age of eight. DeWayne was raised in poverty by an aunt in Baltimore. In high school he worked as a golf caddy at Woodholme Country Club, an all-white Jewish club that he could reach by bus. At age 18, upon becoming the father of a baby girl, he dropped out of high school and enlisted in the Air Force, marrying his girlfriend a year later. He earned his general equivalency high school diploma, was a combat photographer in Vietnam, and returned to Baltimore in 1968. After two years of community college, he earned a journalism degree from the University of Maryland.

Ernest Everett Just
(1883–1941)

"We feel the beauty of nature because we are part of nature."

A pioneering cell biologist. Born in South Carolina, he was four when his father died. His mother taught in an African American school in Charleston and worked in phosphate mines. Having learned to read and write, he had to learn both again after surviving childhood typhoid fever. Sent by his mother at age 16 to a college-preparatory high school in New Hampshire in the hope of a better education than a Southern school for Blacks could provide, Just returned home for a visit to find that his mother had died an hour before his arrival. He completed high school in three years, graduating at the top of his class, then graduated magna cum laude from Dartmouth. Unable to find a faculty position at a white university, he accepted a teaching position at Howard University in 1907. His career research on marine invertebrate eggs (including summers at the Marine Biological Laboratory in Woods Hole, Massachusetts) showed that cell-surface ectoplasm plays a more dynamic role in animal development than previously thought. Discouraged by academic racism in America, he accepted at least ten research appointments in

Europe between 1929 and 1940 and was working in France when the Nazis invaded that country. He was sent to a prisoner-of-war camp but rescued by the US State Department and returned to America, where he died from pancreatic cancer a year later.

Faith Ringgold
(1934–)

"You can't sit around and wait for somebody to say who you are. You need to write it and paint it and do it."

Born in Harlem and raised in New York City during the Harlem Renaissance, Ringgold is a former public school art teacher, artist, writer, painter, performance artist, and professor who uses her art to communicate her political beliefs. The daughter of a fashion designer who taught her how to sew and work with fabrics, she first produced paintings that presented the civil rights movement from a woman's perspective. In the 1970s she lectured at feminist art conferences and actively sought racial integration of the New York art world. In the 1980s she began producing story quilts that combine text, quilting, and painting, one of which was adapted into *Tar Beach* (1991), a Caldecott Honor-winning children's book, and is now in the permanent collection of the Guggenheim Museum in New York

City. Ringgold has written and illustrated more than 17 children's books.

Florence Griffith Joyner
"Flo-Jo"
(1959–1998)

"People don't pay much attention to you when you are second best."

World record holder in the 100-meter and 200-meter sprints, winner of three gold medals at the 1988 Summer Olympics in Seoul, South Korea, she became popular because of her record-setting performances and flashy running outfits and the long, brightly colored fingernails that she wore while competing. The seventh of eleven children, raised by a single mother, she grew up in public housing in the Watts neighborhood of Los Angeles. She started racing at seven, won the Jesse Owens National Youth Games two years in a row, and enrolled at California State University, Northridge, but had to drop out to support her family, working as a bank teller. When her coach, Bob Kersee, found financial aid that would allow her to return to college and athletic competition, she followed him to UCLA in 1980. She won a silver medal in the 200-meter event at the 1984 Olympics in Los Angeles. In 1987 she married Al Joyner, triple-jump gold medalist in 1984. Retiring from competition after the 1988 Olympics, she

passed away from an epileptic seizure ten years later. Her 100- and 200-meter world records still stand.

Frederick Douglass
(1817?–1895)

"Power concedes nothing without a demand. It never did and never will."

Born into slavery from which he ultimately escaped to become one of the most famous intellectuals, orators, authors, and abolitionists of his time. Surreptitiously taught the alphabet by the wife of a family he was "lent" to as a slave, Douglass learned how to read and write with the help of white children in the neighborhood and from newspapers, books, and any materials he could find access to. After escaping slavery in Maryland and moving to New Bedford, Massachusetts, Douglass became an active abolitionist and prolific speaker and published his first autobiography and best-known work, *Narrative of the Life of Frederick Douglass, An American Slave* (1845). Buying his freedom with proceeds from his book, Douglass started an abolitionist newspaper, attended and spoke at the first women's rights convention (the Seneca Falls Convention, where he was the only African American to speak), became an early advocate for school desegregation, advised Presidents Abraham

Lincoln and Andrew Johnson, was the first African American nominated for Vice President of the United States, and served as ambassador to the Dominican Republican, becoming the first Black man to hold a high government position.

"It is easier to build strong children than to repair broken men."

George Washington Carver
(1864–1943)

"I know of nothing more inspiring than that of making discoveries for one's self."

Agricultural scientist, inventor, and educator known for devising peanut products, he was one of most famous African Americans during his lifetime, achieving national and international fame, and was consulted by President Theodore Roosevelt and Mahatma Ghandi on agricultural matters. Born a slave, Carver was freed in 1865 when the Civil War ended slavery in Missouri. Denied admission to college because of his race, Carver conducted biological experiments and sketched botanical samples on his own, eventually becoming the first Black student at Iowa State. After receiving a master's degree and establishing a reputation as a brilliant botanist, he was hired by Booker T. Washington to run Tuskegee Institute's (now Tuskegee University) agricultural department, became the first Black faculty member at his alma mater Iowa State, pioneered traveling schools and outreach programs to provide educational opportunities to farmers, and helped former slaves earn livelihoods by developing and refining new crops.

Gordon Parks
(1912–2006)

"The subject matter is so much more important than the photographer."

Award-winning photojournalist, film director, musician, composer, and author known for his commitment to social justice. His work explores African American culture, race relations, poverty, civil rights, and urban life from the 1940s into the 2000s. Born into poverty, the youngest of fifteen children, he was sent to a live with a sister after his mother died when he was 14, and subsequently supported himself as a waiter, busboy, semipro basketball player, singer, and piano player. At age 25, after seeing photos of migrant workers, he taught himself to use a pawnshop camera and eventually became the first African American staff photographer for *Life* magazine, a position he held for more than two decades. He was also the first African American to write and direct a major Hollywood studio feature film, *The Learning Tree* (1969), and he directed the box office success *Shaft* (1971). His most famous photographs, *American Gothic* (1943) and *Emerging Man* (1952), helped rally support for the burgeoning civil rights movement, and his work is in the permanent collections of many major museums.

Gregory Hines
(1946–2003)

"For me, the feet have always been the thrill."

Actor, choreographer, singer, musician, and one of the most celebrated tap dancers of all time. He began tap-dancing before he was three, turned professional at age five, and grew up backstage at the Apollo Theater in Harlem, where he performed with his brother and father. In his amazingly varied career he won a Tony Award on Broadway (for his performance in *Jelly's Last Jam*), starred in movies such as *The Cotton Club* and *White Nights*, directed films, starred in his own television series, and sang a duet with Luther Vandross called "There's Nothing Better Than Love," which reached #1 on the Billboard R&B charts.

Guion S. Bluford Jr.
(1942–)

"I've come to appreciate the planet we live on. It's a small ball in a large universe. It's a very fragile ball but also very beautiful. You don't recognize that until you see it from a little farther off."

Aerospace engineer, decorated US Air Force pilot, and the first African American to travel into space. Born in Philadelphia, Pennsylvania, to a mechanical engineer and a special education teacher, the oldest of three sons, he received a BS in aerospace engineering from Pennsylvania State University in 1964, then flew 144 combat missions for the Air Force, 65 of them over North Vietnam. He earned MS and PhD degrees from the Air Force Institute of Technology and was selected for the NASA astronaut training program in 1978, participating in four Space Shuttle flights between 1983 and 1992 and logging 688 hours in space.

Gwen Ifill
(1955–2016)

"Change comes from listening, learning, caring, and conversation."

Journalist and author. Born in Queens, New York, daughter of an African Methodist Episcopal minister who moved his family from church to church throughout the Northeast when Gwen was growing up. Graduated from Simmons College in Boston in 1977 with a BA in communications and reported for the *Boston Herald-American*, the *Baltimore Evening Sun*, the *Washington Post* (1984–1991), and the *New York Times* (1991–1994), where she covered the White House. She moved to television as NBC's Capitol Hill reporter in 1994, and in 1999 became the first Black woman to host a nationally aired public affairs program as moderator of PBS's *Washington Week in Review*. She also became co-anchor and co-managing editor of *PBS NewsHour*, moderated vice-presidential debates in 2004 and 2008, and wrote the bestselling book *The Breakthrough: Politics and Race in the Age of Obama* (2009).

Harriet Ross Tubman
"Moses"
(1820?–1913)

"I was the conductor of the Underground Railroad for eight years, and I can say what most conductors can't say — I never ran my train off the track and I never lost a passenger."

Most widely known for her work ferrying hundreds of slaves northward on the Underground Railroad without losing a single passenger to capture, Harriet Tubman was also a celebrated scout, spy, and nurse for the Union Army. Born a slave around 1820 on a plantation in Maryland, her own Underground Railroad journey began in 1849 when she set off for Philadelphia after

hearing a rumor that she was to be sold. Undeterred by the difficulties she faced, Tubman made that treacherous trip at least 19 times by 1860, devising ingenious methods to outsmart slave hunters and the press and using her determination and stern discipline to motivate the weary fugitives under her care to press on toward freedom.

Harry Belafonte
(1927–)

"If I've impacted one heart, one mind, one soul, and brought to that individual a greater truth than that individual came into a relationship with me having, then I would say that I have been successful."

Known as the King of Calypso, Harold George Belafonte brought music from his Caribbean roots to an American audience, recording the first album to sell over one million copies. With numerous appearances on screen and stage, Belafonte's charismatic presence has won him Tony, Emmy, and Grammy awards. Amid the turmoil of the civil rights movement of the 1960s, Belafonte became the first Black man to win an Emmy and the first to be credited as a television producer, where his work positioned Black sounds and stories as important forces for change. Throughout his career, Belafonte has placed his star

power behind sit-ins in the American South and anti-apartheid and famine-abatement movements in South Africa, rallying Hollywood around the project of equality.

Henry Louis Gates Jr.
(1950–)

"The story of the African American people is the story of the settlement and growth of America itself, a universal tale that all people should experience."

Scholar, filmmaker, literary critic, and recipient of 55 honorary degrees whose work examines the ways Black Americans have used literature to indirectly reference oppressive structures in a practice called "signifyin'." He traces this practice, present in the work of prominent authors from Alice Walker to Zora Neale Hurston, back to a trickster figure in Yoruba mythology named Esu. The first Black man to be awarded the National Humanities Medal, Gates advocates for the close study and rightful inclusion of Black American literature in the Western literary canon. Gates has applied the methods developed for his "literary archaeology" to the screen as well, using documentary television to share stories from all corners of the African diaspora.

Ida Bell Wells-Barnett
(1862–1931)

"The people must know before they can act, and there is no educator to compare with the press."

Born into slavery in Mississippi, she was freed by the Emancipation Proclamation when two months old. Her father was a successful carpenter, her mother a cook. At the age of 16 she lost both parents to yellow fever; she became a teacher at a Black elementary school, and later moved to Memphis with two younger sisters, where they lived with an aunt and Ida found a teaching job and took college classes at Fisk University. In 1884 she was ordered out of her seat in a train's first-class ladies' car, then forcibly removed from the train when she resisted. She won a suit against the railroad in lower court, but the verdict was reversed by the Tennessee Supreme Court and she was forced to pay court costs. She took to journalism as a way to document and publicize Jim Crow oppression in the South. Her articles and editorials about lynchings led to the 1892 destruction by a white mob of the offices of the newspaper she co-owned. Out of town at the time, she was spared personal harm and continued her anti-lynching writing from New York and then Chicago, marrying civil-rights activist, journalist, and lawyer Ferdinand Barnett in 1895. Her founding and leadership of organizations like the Negro Fellowship League and the Alpha Suffrage Club, one of the first Black women's suffrage groups, enacted her belief that Black Americans must design their own pathways to the equality they deserve. Outspoken and unbending, she was admired and supported by Frederick Douglass but sometimes at odds with Booker T. Washington and W.E.B. Du Bois, who became the leading African American voices after Douglass's death in 1895 (and who were often at odds with each other). She wrote in her autobiography (*Crusade for Justice*, published posthumously) that Du Bois deliberately excluded her from the list of founders of the NAACP.

Jackie Robinson
(1919–1972)

"A life is not important except in the impact it has on other lives."

Jack Roosevelt Robinson used the common ground of baseball to confront racism in America. After growing up in poverty, his exceptional athleticism gained him notoriety at UCLA, where he was the first student to win varsity letters in four sports. Drafted into the Army in 1942, Robinson was assigned to a Black cavalry unit but was disciplined during training for refusing to sit in the back of a supposedly unsegregated bus. Although he was acquitted in a court martial, the incident prevented him from combat duty in World War II. He became the first Black player to join the Brooklyn Dodgers, marking a milestone for the integration of sports. Despite enduring vitriol from the public and even his own team members, Robinson was determined to stand as proof that Black Americans were equals on and off the field. He was the National League Rookie of the Year in 1947, a six-time Major League All-Star from 1949–1954, and was voted into the Baseball Hall of Fame in 1962. He lent his voice as a spokesperson for the NAACP and was a prominent member of the civil rights movement; he received a Congressional Gold Medal and a Presidential Medal of Freedom after his death at the age of 53.

Jacob Armstead Lawrence
(1917–2000)

"I am part of the Black community, so I am the Black community speaking."

An artist of the Harlem Renaissance, Jacob Lawrence told stories through series of paintings. Characterized by vibrant colors and forms filled with motion and purpose, his work used a historiographic approach to depict the vitality and resilience of the Black community. Lawrence exhibited his most popular work, the *Migration Series*, at the age of 24, a sequence of sixty paintings chronicling the ongoing Great Migration away from the Jim Crow South. His success continued from there; Lawrence was the first Black artist to be included in the Museum of Modern Art's permanent collection and one of the first to be honored with a solo retrospective on his work. Until the end of his life, Lawrence continued to paint and teach at art schools in New York, Washington, and North Carolina.

James Baldwin
(1924–1987)

"You think your pain and heartbreak are unprecedented in the history of the world, but then you read."

Through novels including *Go Tell It on the Mountain* (1953), essays such as those collected in *Notes of a Native Son* (1955) and *The Fire Next Time* (1963), and his plays, poems, and short stories, Baldwin endeavored to share the joy and pain of the Black experience in America. Born and raised in Harlem, grandson of a slave, his stepfather a Baptist preacher who treated him harshly, Baldwin grew up poor, escaping into libraries and literature. "I knew I was black, of course, but I also knew I was smart," he wrote in *Notes of a Native Son*. "I didn't know how I would use my mind, or even if I could, but that was the only thing I had to use." For a few teenaged years he developed his voice and worldview as a Pentecostal junior preacher, but he left the church at age 17. Disillusioned with America's racism, struggling with his growing realization of his homosexuality, he moved to Paris at age 24 and lived in France for most of his remaining life. "I think my exile saved my life," he wrote, "for it inexorably confirmed something which Americans appear to have great difficulty accepting. Which is, simply, this: a man is not a man until he is able and willing to accept his own vision of the world, no matter how radically this vision departs from others." Feeling a moral imperative to add his voice and presence to the Black struggle for justice in America, he returned in the summer of 1957. His writing shone a light on the corrosive effects of racism on haters as well as the hated, highlighting the faulty logic of white supremacy and encouraging Black Americans to take personal education and identity formation seriously.

"We are responsible for the world in which we find ourselves, if only because we are the only sentient force which can change it."
–from *No Name in the Street*

"Our crown has already been bought and paid for. All we have to do is wear it." –quoted in Toni Morrison's eulogy for Baldwin

"Not everything that is faced can be changed; but nothing can be changed until it is faced."

Jay-Z
(1969–)

"You learn more in failure than you ever do in success."

Born Shawn Corey Carter, one of four siblings raised by his mother in a housing project in the Bedford-Stuyvesant neighborhood of Brooklyn, never finishing high school, Jay-Z emerged as one of New York's most popular rappers in the late 1990s. An occasional backup for rapper acquaintances, he co-founded Roc-A-Fella Records in 1995 after failing to secure a record deal from a major label. His first album, *Reasonable Doubt* (1996), eventually went platinum, as did the follow-up album, *In My Lifetime, Vol. 1* (1997), produced by Sean "Puff Daddy" Combs and distributed by Def Jam Recordings. His continued run of successful albums and singles led to his appointment as president of Def Jam in 2004. He has sold more than 50 million albums and 75 million singles and has won 22 Grammy Awards. A businessman and entrepreneur, he has built companies and brands, bought sports teams, and founded lifestyle and recording label Roc Nation in 2008. In 2017 he became the first rapper to be inducted into the Songwriters Hall of Fame. He became a billionaire in 2019. As his wealth grows, so does his commitment to philanthropy; along with his wife, Beyoncé, Jay-Z continues to invest in prison reform and supports victims of police brutality through the Shawn Carter Foundation.

Jean-Michel Basquiat
(1960–1988)

"If you wanna talk about influence, man, then you've got to realize that influence is not influence. It's simply someone's idea going through my new mind."

Brooklyn-born artist who elevated graffiti to a startling Expressionist artform; his 1982 painting *Untitled* sold for $110.5 million at a 2017 Sotheby's auction, a record for an American artist's work. His father was Haitian, his mother of Puerto Rican descent; she took her young son to New York art museums and enrolled him as a junior member of the Brooklyn Art Museum. He learned to read and write by age four, was fluent in French, English, and Spanish by age 11, but never finished high school. His home life was unstable, his mother having been committed to a psychiatric hospital when he was 13. In 1976 he and a friend began spray painting buildings in Lower Manhattan under the pseudonym SAMO, with countercultural messages that expressed his frustration with the city's poverty and instability. His art career took off in 1980 when his work was included in the Times Square Show; critics raved about his unique style that combined street art with influences from abstract expressionism and pop-art. Under the mentorship of celebrity artists like Keith Haring and Andy Warhol, Basquiat used text and skeletal figures to create intense diagrams illustrating the contentious forces at play in a rapidly changing society and his own transforming identity. He created an astonishing volume of work before dying of a drug overdose at age 27. Even as his popularity soared, Basquiat maintained that art did not belong to the rich or the educated but was a vital means of expression.

"I don't know anybody who needs a critic to find out what art is."

Jerry Pinkney
(1939–)

"I want kids to understand that making pictures is similar to making music; there are so many instruments and so many tunes that the possibilities for how you play are truly limitless."

Beloved artist and children's book illustrator whose work has comforted and inspired readers of all ages. Influenced by classic folktales and fables, Pinkney uses his art to depict diverse families and strong role models on greeting cards, album covers, and magazines as well as his most beloved form, book illustrations. Since his first children's book, *The Adventures of Spider: West African Folk Tales* (1964), he has illustrated more than 100 others, in recent decades often creating the text as well—not bad for someone who struggled with dyslexia as a kid in Philadelphia. His work has received five Coretta Scott King awards, a Caldecott Medal (*The Lion & the Mouse*, 2009) and five Caldecott Honors, an Orbis Pictus Award (*A Place to Land: Martin Luther King Jr. and the Speech that Inspired a Nation*, 2019), and many other recognitions. He advocates for arts programs that encourage creative expression as a tool to understand and relate to the world.

Jesse Owens
(1913–1980)

"I always loved running—it was something you could do by yourself and under your own power."

Track and field star whose four gold medals at the 1936 Olympic Games in Berlin exposed the emptiness of the Nazi myth of Aryan supremacy. The youngest of ten children born to an Alabama sharecropper, James Cleveland Owens moved north to Cleveland with his family when he was nine, part of the Great Migration. When he told a teacher his name was J.C., she heard Jesse, and the name stuck. Ironically, though Hitler congratulated him for his Olympic performances, President Franklin Roosevelt never did, and Jesse was forced to ride the freight elevator to his own celebratory reception at the Waldorf Astoria Hotel in New York. Largely left out of the sponsorships and opportunities offered to other medal winners, Owens pieced together a hand-to-mouth existence working blue collar jobs and demonstrating his foot speed for money. After filing for bankruptcy in 1966, he made a way for himself as a magnanimous public speaker, and later as an ambassador for the US State Department. His legacy continues to inspire track athletes in America and beyond. The secret of his speed, he said, was simple:

"I let my feet spend as little time on the ground as possible. From the air, fast down, and from the ground, fast up."

Jesse Jackson
(1941–)

"Our dreams must be stronger than our memories. We must be pulled by our dreams, rather than pushed by our memories."

Born to a single 16-year-old mother in Greenville, South Carolina, Jesse Louis Jackson came to consider both his biological father and his stepfather (whose surname he was given) as fathers. He attended the University of Illinois on a football scholarship but transferred to North Carolina A&T, where he played quarterback and was elected student body president. After college he attended Chicago Divinity School but dropped out just short of earning his degree. He was ordained as a minister in 1968. He joined the Selma to Montgomery marches in 1965, and his penchant for organizing led Dr. King to appoint him national director of the Southern Christian Leadership Conference's economic arm, Operation Breadbasket, in 1967. Despite numerous successes in that role, Jackson was suspended from the directorship in 1971 by King's successor as chairman of the SCLC, Ralph Abernathy, with whom he clashed. He immediately founded Operation PUSH (People United to Serve Humanity) to improve economic opportunities for Blacks and the poor. He made his first bid for the Democratic presidential nomination in 1984,

placing third, the best showing to that time by a Black presidential candidate. He ran again in 1988, doubling his primary vote and placing second. His platform both times included a single-payer health care system, free community college for all, reversing the Reagan-era tax cuts for the wealthy (and using the revenues to finance social welfare programs), and rebuilding America's infrastructure with a public works program like those of the 1930s. He founded the Rainbow Coalition for social justice (for the poor and for all who suffer discrimination) after his 1984 presidential run; it merged with Operation PUSH in 1996. Jackson's skill as a public speaker and natural motivator have made him an important figure in the struggle for justice.

"Never look down on somebody unless you're helping them up."

Jim Brown
(1936–)

"Success is not only for the elite. Success is there for those that want it, plan for it, and take action to achieve it."

Widely considered the greatest American football player of all time, James Nathaniel Brown was born on St. Simons Island, Georgia, but went to high school on Long Island, New York, where he was a multisport star

athlete. He excelled in football, basketball, track, and lacrosse at Syracuse University and was selected by the Cleveland Browns in the 1957 draft, the sixth player chosen. A uniquely talented and durable running back, Brown was Rookie of the Year in 1957 and earned three Most Valuable Player designations and nine Pro Bowl invitations in his nine seasons, never missing a game. His 2,359 carries, 12,312 rushing yards, and 106 touchdowns were all records at the time of his 1966 retirement; he was inducted into the NFL Hall of Fame in 1971. He began acting in 1964 and has accumulated a long list of film and television credits. Despite a turbulent private life, including assault charges and jail time, he has campaigned for racial equality and worked to quell gang violence in Los Angeles.

"There were a lot of running backs as good as me. The real difference was that I could focus. I never laid back and relied on natural ability."

Jimi Hendrix
(1942–1970)

"All I play is truth and emotion."

Born in Seattle, James Marshall Hendrix was the oldest of five siblings and had a difficult childhood. His parents divorced when he was nine; he and a brother remained in his father's custody. He did not graduate from high school. Acquiring his first guitar (acoustic) at age 15, he practiced incessantly and listened to blues recordings. At age 19 he joined the Army and was assigned to paratrooper training; discharged after a year, he embarked on a three-year apprenticeship as an itinerant guitarist, during which he backed Wilson Pickett, Sam Cooke, the Isley Brothers, and Little Richard, among others. In 1966 he was introduced to Chas Chandler, the former bassist for the Animals, who became his manager in London, convinced him to change Jimmy to Jimi, and recruited the other two members of the Jimi Hendrix Experience. Though Hendrix could neither read nor write music, his star power and musical innovations continue to influence the most popular musical artists today. He is most known for songs such as "Hey Joe," "Purple Haze," and "The Wind Cries Mary" that melded soul, jazz, rock, blues, and early electronica to create a unique sound that pushed the limits of the electric guitar. The band's three albums—*Are You Experienced, Axis: Bold as Love*, and *Electric Ladyland*—have been ranked by *Rolling Stone* among the 100 greatest albums of all time; *Rolling Stone* ranks Hendrix the greatest guitarist of all time. His untimely death from an accidental drug overdose at 28 ended his meteoric career.

"If there is something to be changed in this world then it can only happen with music."

Jimmy Winkfield
"Wink"
(1882–1974)

"To be a great jockey, you have to have a stopwatch in your head."

A shoeshine boy in Lexington, Kentucky, he became a champion jockey—winning the Kentucky Derby twice by age 20—on the cusp of the takeover of the sport by white Southerners. Blackballed by stable owners, wary of threats from other jockeys and the Ku Klux Klan, Winkfield traveled to Europe in 1904. He quickly became the Russian National Riding Champion and collected accolades from across the continent. Imperiled by the tumult of the Russian Revolution, he led fellow horsemen and more than 200 thoroughbreds on a 1,100-mile trek to safety in Poland. Two decades later he was at the top of the sport in France, living large, when the Nazi invasion forced him to flee again. In his sixties he wielded a jackhammer with his 105-pound frame on the streets of Queens for the Works Progress Administration. In his seventies he reestablished himself as a top French trainer and stable owner. His legacy of more than 2,600 career wins remained largely unknown before he was inducted into America's Racing Hall of Fame thirty years after his death.

Joan Higginbotham
(1964–)

"I just feel a sense of responsibility... for people who are coming up."

Engineer and astronaut, began her NASA career just two weeks after graduating from college. She participated in 53 shuttle launches in the first nine years of her career, working in many areas of shuttle design, construction, and maintenance. Her skill and kind leadership in areas from operations support and communications to robotics led NASA to invite her to train as an astronaut. In 2006, Higginbotham became the third Black woman to fly into space, where she participated in the construction of the International Space Station. She logged over 308 hours of spacetime before retiring from her distinguished 30-year career to continue work in the private sector as an advocate for education.

Joe Louis
(1914–1981)

"A champion doesn't become a champion in the ring, he's merely recognized in the ring. His 'becoming' happens during his daily routine."

Born in rural Alabama, Joseph Louis Barrow moved to Detroit with his family in 1926, part of the Great Migration. There he discovered amateur boxing despite his mother's desire that he play the violin; he may have shortened his name to hide his fighting from her. He turned professional in 1934, won the world heavyweight championship with a knockout of James Braddock in 1937, and successfully defended his title 25 times (21 by knockout) before his initial retirement in 1949—the longest championship reign in any weight class. His 1938 bout with German champion Max Schmeling (who had beaten Louis in 1936) was framed by the media as a battle between Nazism and American democracy; Louis scored a technical knockout in just over two minutes. His precision and tenacity in the ring were balanced by a genteel personality outside it, an image that set him apart as a symbol of Black power and an example of what Black Americans could achieve if given an opportunity. Interrupted by Army service in World War II, he retired with a stunning record of 68 wins and 54 knockouts over 17 years. His attempted comeback for financial reasons was halted by a loss to Rocky Marciano, but friends came to his financial aid, including his old foe Schmeling.

John Carlos
(1945–)

"How can you ask someone to live in the world and not have something to say about injustice?"

Born and raised in Harlem, a high school and college track star, John Wesley Carlos is most known for his demonstration at the 1968 Summer Olympics with teammate Tommie Smith to protest America's treatment of Black Americans. After winning the bronze medal in the 200-meter sprint, Carlos and Smith (the gold medal-winner) stood barefoot on the podium, and each raised a fist covered by a black glove. Carlos described the poverty and daily discrimination his family had faced in internationally broadcasted interviews after the protest. Avery Brundage, whose removal from the presidency of the International Olympic Committee was one of Carlos and Smith's objectives, forced the US Olympic Committee to expel the athletes from the games. Carlos tied the world 100-yard record in 1969 before retiring from running; after a professional football career was aborted by injury, he worked a series of dead-end jobs before becoming a guidance counselor and track coach at Palm Springs High School in California. In 2006, Carlos and Smith were pallbearers at the funeral of Peter Norman, the white

Australian sprinter who won the silver medal that day in 1968 and wore an Olympic Project for Human Rights badge in the awards ceremony to show his support for the protest.

John Hope Franklin
(1915–2009)

"My challenge was to weave into the fabric of American history enough of the presence of Blacks so that the story of the United States could be told adequately and fairly."

Author of the seminal work *From Slavery to Freedom* (1947), which has sold more than three million copies, and a prolific historian and scholar of the Civil War era. Over the course of his career, Franklin published 116 essays and more than 75 longer works that helped define, establish, and grow the field of African American studies. He was born in Oklahoma, son of an attorney who defended African American survivors of the 1921 Tulsa race riot, in which at least 26 Black Americans were killed, hundreds were injured, and dozens of Black-owned businesses were burned or destroyed. John held positions at Brooklyn College, University of Chicago, Duke University, and other prestigious institutions, and he served on numerous committees and advisory boards that sought solutions to racial inequalities in America. He worked

with Thurgood Marshall and the NAACP Legal Defense Fund to prepare the legal case for Brown v. Board of Education. He was awarded the Presidential Medal of Freedom in 1995.

John Lewis
(1940–2020)

"Change often takes time. It rarely happens all at once."

The son of Alabama sharecroppers, he became a central figure in the American civil rights movement, adopting a nonviolent struggle against systemic racism as his life's work. Inspired by Rosa Parks and the Montgomery bus boycott, he met Martin Luther King Jr. in 1958 and started getting into what he called "trouble, good trouble, necessary trouble." His first arrest came in February 1960 for demanding service at whites-only lunch counters in Nashville, a sit-in that led to his founding and early leadership of the Student Nonviolent Coordinating Committee. He would be arrested 39 more times before the end of 1966. In 1961 he was one of the thirteen original Freedom Riders (seven Black students, six white) who rode Greyhound and Trailways buses south from Washington, DC to call attention to illegal segregation on interstate buses; he was beaten unconscious outside the Greyhound terminal in Montgomery. He

helped organize the 1963 March on Washington and was one of the speakers there, shoulder to shoulder with Dr. King. In March 1965—on what became known as Bloody Sunday—he led the historic march in Selma and was so severely beaten by Alabama state troopers that his skull was cracked; televised images of the beatings of Lewis and others galvanized support for the Voting Rights Act, which President Lyndon Johnson presented to Congress eight days later. Elected to Congress in 1986, representing Atlanta, Lewis compiled a progressive voting record and became known as "the conscience of the Congress." Before his death in 2020, he lent his support to the Black Lives Matter movement, saying,

"This feels and looks so different. There will be no turning back."

Josephine Baker
(1906–1975)

"One day I realized I was living in a country where I was afraid to be black. It was only a country for white people. Not black. So I left. I had been suffocating in the United States.... A lot of us left, not because we wanted to leave, but because we couldn't stand it anymore.... I felt liberated in Paris."

Born in St. Louis as Freda Josephine McDonald, to a poor single mother. Poorly clothed, often hungry, she dropped out of school at age 12 and lived on the streets, working as a waitress and dancing for spare change. She married Willie Baker at age 15 (her first marriage, at 13, having lasted less than a year), and though she divorced him within a few years, she used the name Baker for the rest of her life. Later in 1921, thanks in part to the Harlem Renaissance, she was booked to dance in New York City vaudeville and Broadway revues. She sailed to France in 1925, appearing in La Revue Négre at Paris's Théâtre des Champs-Élysées and quickly becoming a star, selling out live shows in the city's largest theaters and adding an alluring singing voice to her dancing. She was a celebrated icon of the Jazz Age and appeared in several films. When World War II broke out, Baker became a spy for the French Resistance, reporting (from Paris and later Morocco) information she learned while attending embassy and ministry gatherings; she was decorated for this work by the postwar French government. Outraged by racism and segregation she encountered upon returning to the US for a national tour of sold-out performances in 1951, she crusaded for civil rights and was honored for her work by the NAACP. In 1963, she was the only woman invited to speak at Dr. King's famous March on Washington, where she said:

"I have walked into the palaces of kings and queens and into the houses of presidents. And much more. But I could not walk into a hotel in America and get a cup of coffee, and that made me mad. And when I get mad, you know that I open my big mouth. And then look out, 'cause when Josephine opens her mouth, they hear it all over the world."

Judith Jamison
(1943–)

"Maybe it's a generational thing, but I never wanted to be the best Black dancer in the world. I just wanted to be the best."

A versatile dancer and choreographer, Jamison's career took off in 1965 when she joined the Alvin Ailey American Dance Theater, dancing in Ailey's signature works *Blues Suite* and *Revelations*, among others. Best known for her performance of Ailey's renowned 16-minute solo dance work *Cry* (1971)—created for "all black women everywhere, especially our mothers"—Jamison proved herself a profoundly expressive dancer. She took her talents to stages around the world, including the Broadway musical *Sophisticated Ladies* (1981–1983), and choreographed for her own dance company, The Jamison Project, before returning in 1989 to succeed Ailey as the Dance Theater's second artistic director, becoming the first Black woman to direct a major modern dance company. She continued in this position for 21 years and continued dancing, traveling for coveted performances at national ballets from Stockholm to Vienna. Her autobiography, *Dancing Spirit*, was published in 1993. Jamison exalts dance as a way to tell stories that celebrate Black histories and futures.

"People came to see beauty and I danced to give it to them."

Kareem Abdul-Jabbar
(1947–)

"My biggest resource is my mind."

Born Ferdinand Lewis Alcindor Jr., one of the greatest basketball players of all time, a towering (7 feet 2 inches) center known for his unblockable "skyhook," which he could shoot with either hand. Elected to the Naismith Memorial Basketball Hall of Fame, he is the National Basketball Association's all-time leading scorer; he won six NBA titles, six NBA Most Valuable Player awards, and two NBA Finals MVP awards and was a 19-time NBA All-Star in his 20 seasons, the first six with the Milwaukee Bucks and the last 14 with the Los Angeles Lakers. He won three college national championships at UCLA and was so good coming out of high school in New York City that college basketball made dunking illegal, fearing he would dominate the game. He practiced yoga and martial arts to increase his flexibility and prolong his professional basketball career. Introverted by nature, his stand-offish press relations may have stymied his post-retirement coaching aspirations. He has acted in film and television; has written, directed, produced, and narrated Black history documentaries; is a best-selling author; and has spoken out on issues involving race, religion, and inequality. He was nominated for an Emmy Award for his narration in the documentary special *Black Patriots: Heroes of The Revolution* and received the Presidential Medal of Freedom in 2016.

"The existence of racism in America isn't an opinion. It's a quantifiable fact."

Katherine Johnson
(1918–2020)

"Girls are capable of doing everything men are capable of doing."

Mathematician who worked at NASA and was instrumental in the success of the Apollo 11 moon mission, the Space Shuttle program, and the Earth Resources Satellite. She demonstrated a gift for academics and numbers early in life, graduating from eighth grade by the age of 10 and high school at age 14. The daughter of Joylette Roberta Lowe, a teacher, and Joshua McKinley Coleman, who worked as a farmer and janitor among other jobs, she enrolled at West Virginia State College (now West Virginia State University), where she was taught by Dr. William W. Schieffelin Claytor, the third African American to earn a PhD in mathematics, and graduated summa cum laude at age 18 with degrees in mathematics and French. One of the first African American women to work as a NASA scientist, she helped pioneer the use of computers to perform the complex calculations used in space travel. The film *Hidden Figures* (2017) was based on the lives of Johnson and other African American mathematicians at NASA.

Kendrick Lamar
(1987–)

"My whole thing is to inspire, to better people, to better myself forever in this thing we call rap, this thing we call hip-hop."

Kendrick Lamar Duckworth is a rapper and hip-hop artist whose album *Damn* (2017) won the Pulitzer Prize for Music and whose soundtrack for the movie *Black Panther* (2018) won Academy and Grammy awards for best original score. He has won thirteen Grammy Awards to date and is considered one of the most talented rappers of his generation. Born in the Los Angeles metropolitan city of Compton, he grew up poor, his parents on welfare and food stamps, surrounded by gang violence. Afflicted by a stutter until middle school, he was turned onto poetry in seventh grade by an English teacher; he started writing and never looked back.

Langston Hughes
(1902–1967)

My People

The stars are beautiful,

So the eyes of my people.

Beautiful, also, is the sun.

Beautiful, also, are the souls of my people.

(1923, from The Crisis)

Poet, playwright, novelist, and columnist; innovator who wrote "jazz poetry"; a central figure in the Harlem Renaissance. James Mercer Langston Hughes was born in Joplin, Missouri, and lived in six different cities by the time he was 12. He worked as a farmer, a cook, a waiter, a sailor, a Paris nightclub doorman; he graduated from college; he traveled in Latin America, West Africa, and Europe. He wrote from wide experience and a zesty appreciation of the people he met. Many of his short pieces featured a fictional character, Jesse B. Semple (or Simple), who gave voice to the problems of a poor Black man in a racist society; general readers loved him. He wrote for *The Crisis*, the NAACP magazine; he wrote a weekly column for *The Chicago Defender* from 1942 to 1962; he wrote children's books, plays, and a dozen novels and short story collections. First and last, until his death in 1967, he wrote poetry—a dozen volumes of it, beginning with *The Weary Blues* (1926) and including "Harlem" (1951), which helped inspire Lorraine Hansberry's play *A Raisin in the Sun*:

What happens to a dream deferred?

Does it dry up

like a raisin in the sun?

Or fester like a sore—

And then run?

...Maybe it just sags

Like a heavy load.

Or does it explode?

Laurence Fishburne
(1961–)

"It's not that I take myself seriously; I take what I do seriously."

Stage and screen actor whose credits include *Boyz N the Hood* (1991*), What's Love Got to Do With It* (1993), *Othello* (1995), *The Matrix* trilogy, and *Two Trains Running* (1990), for which he received a Tony Award. Producer, playwright, screenwriter, and film director. Born in Augusta, Georgia, and raised in Brooklyn, New York; graduated from Lincoln Square Academy in New York. He already had experience in TV and movies when at 14 he lied about his age and landed a role in *Apocalypse Now*; by the time it was finished he was 17, as he'd claimed in the beginning. He has won awards for roles as different as Morpheus (in *Matrix*, 2000) and Thurgood Marshall (in the one-man Broadway play *Thurgood*, 2008).

Lisa Leslie
(1972–)

"I encourage girls to play sports and play hard."

WNBA basketball player, four-time Olympic gold medalist, three-time WNBA MVP, and first player to dunk in a WNBA game. Inducted into the Naismith Basketball Hall of Fame. Six feet tall in middle school, she was annoyed when people asked if she played basketball but fell in love with the game. She played for the Los Angeles Sparks (1997–2009). She and husband Michael Lockwood have a daughter (Lauren Jolie, b. 2007) and a son (Michael Joseph Lockwood II, b. 2010). A model and actress, she also has an MBA (2009) and is an investor in her beloved team, the Sparks.

Lorraine Hansberry
(1930–1965)

"One cannot live with sighted eyes and feeling heart and not know or react to the miseries which afflict this world."

Writer and playwright; her award-winning *A Raisin in the Sun* (1959) was the first play by an African American woman performed on Broadway and has been widely read, taught, and produced ever since. *The Sign in Sidney Brustein's Window* (1964) has also been called a masterpiece; a critique of white liberal self-delusion, it merits much more attention. Hansberry died young of cancer, but not before making her mark. In 1963, Robert Kennedy met with Black intellectual leaders to discuss the situation in Birmingham. Hansberry scolded him for failing to see racial injustice as a moral problem, not merely a social one. Then she walked out on him. Within the month his brother, President John F. Kennedy, delivered a speech that laid the groundwork for the Civil Rights Act, pointing to a moral as well as a legal imperative for civil rights.

Louis Armstrong

"Satchelmouth" or "Satchmo"
(1901–1971)

"Never play anything the same way twice."

Jazz trumpet player, composer, vocalist, and actor. One of the most influential jazz musicians in history, Armstrong was born and raised in the tough "Battlefield" neighborhood of New Orleans and learned to play his cornet while an inmate at the "Colored Waifs Home." He was

mentored by Joe "King" Oliver and played on riverboats before moving to Chicago and New York. Playing with legendary jazz performers, he became one of the greatest jazz legends. He acted in movies with Bing Crosby, Grace Kelly, and other stars, and he remembered early kindnesses. He told Cab Calloway that his style of scat singing came from orthodox Jewish chanting; as a boy, he was helped by a family of Lithuanian Jews, and he wore a Star of David all his life. Some criticized him for not using his popularity with whites to advance the cause of civil rights. He did take a public stand in the 1957 Little Rock crisis, and the FBI kept a file on him for his outspoken support of integration. Irrepressible, gregarious, and incredibly talented, he gave zest and warmth to the jazz scene.

"We all do 'do, re, mi,' but you have got to find the other notes yourself."

Lynn Nottage
(1964–)

"If you lead with anger, it will turn off the audience."

American playwright and professor; the only African American woman to have won two Pulitzer Prizes for Drama, in 2009 for *Ruined* (about Congolese women working to survive in a war zone) and in 2017 for *Sweat* (about longtime factory

friends whose mutual trust is threatened by layoffs). Born in Brooklyn, the daughter of a school principal and a psychologist, she wrote her first full-length play (about an African American Shakespeare company touring the South) in high school. Awarding her a Genius Grant in 2007, the MacArthur Foundation observed her use of "unexpected vantage points" to address "some of society's most complex issues with empathy and humor." She and her husband, director Tony Gerber, founded production company Market Road Films in 2003. She teaches playwriting at Columbia University.

"I am interested in people living in the margins of society, and I do have a mission to tell the stories of women of color in particular. I feel we've been present throughout history, but our voices have been neglected."

Mae Jemison
(1956–)

"Never be limited by other people's limited imaginations."

Astronaut, physician, first African American woman to travel into space. Born in Alabama and raised in Chicago, where an uncle introduced her to science. Double-majored in chemical engineering and Afro-American studies at Stanford; earned her MD from Cornell (1981); and has

practiced medicine in a Cambodian refugee camp, with the Peace Corps in West Africa, and in Los Angeles. Completed NASA astronaut training in 1988 and entered space in 1992 as a mission specialist on the shuttle *Endeavor*. Left NASA in 1993 to found a technology research company. She works to get minority students interested in science and to close the health care gap between the United States and developing nations.

Malcolm X
(1925–1965)

"You can't separate peace from freedom because no one can be at peace unless he has his freedom."

Powerful and brilliant orator and one of the most prominent advocates for Black liberation in the United States in the twentieth century. Born in Omaha as Malcolm Little; later named Malik el-Shabazz. As a teen he spent time in the foster care system, and later turned to crime. In prison he was converted to the Nation of Islam (NOI), a political and religious movement that has been criticized by some for promoting Black supremacist beliefs, and won many converts by his charismatic speaking; media took notice when he intervened after the police beating of an NOI member. He left NOI to become a Sunni Muslim, and in 1964 made his Hajj—his pilgrimage to Mecca, where the interactions of Muslims of "all colors, from blue-eyed blonds to black-skinned Africans," made him think Islam could be a means to overcoming racial division. He became increasingly eager to work with other civil rights leaders, even as his conflict with the NOI intensified. In February 1965 he told an interviewer the NOI was trying to kill him. Two days later he was assassinated before a speech in a Manhattan ballroom.

"If you have no critics, you'll likely have no success."

Marcus Garvey
(1887–1940)

"A people without the knowledge of their past history, origin and culture is like a tree without roots."

Founder of the Universal Negro Improvement Association (UNIA) in 1914, the largest organization that has ever been dedicated to Black economic self-reliance, political self-determination, and racial pride. The UNIA famously advocated for the return to and founding of a Black nation in Africa. Born in Jamaica, Garvey moved to the US in 1916, organized a UNIA chapter in Harlem, and founded a shipping line to connect the Pan-African world, but was ultimately imprisoned and deported back to Jamaica; he later moved to England. At odds with many civil rights leaders (he even worked with the Ku Klux Klan, which shared his belief in racial segregation), he helped launch the "black is beautiful" ideal and in 1964 was declared Jamaica's first national hero.

"With confidence, you have won before you have started."

"We are going to emancipate ourselves from mental slavery, for though others may free the body, none but ourselves can free the mind."

Marian Anderson
(1897?–1993)

"When I sing, I don't want to them to see that my face is black; I don't want them to see that my face is white—I want them to see my soul. And that is colorless."

Award-winning singer who performed a wide range of music and was the first African American to perform at the Metropolitan Opera. Poverty limited Anderson's childhood opportunities in Philadelphia, but her pastor and church raised money to put her through high school and pay for singing lessons. Doors opened after she won a 1925 singing competition sponsored by the New York Philharmonic, and she became successful both in the US and Europe. The most famous moment in her career was in 1939, when the Daughters of the American Revolution refused to let her sing to a multiracial audience in Constitution Hall. Eleanor Roosevelt dropped her DAR membership, President Franklin Roosevelt pulled strings, and Marian Anderson subsequently sang from the steps of the Lincoln Memorial to an audience of 75,000 people while millions more listened by radio. She went on to sing for servicemen in World War II and the Korean War, concertgoers at the Metropolitan Opera, and citizens at two presidential inaugurations (Eisenhower's and Kennedy's) before retiring in 1965 as one of the best-loved singers in America.

Marie Maynard Daly
(1921–2003)

"Courage is like—it's a habitus, a habit, a virtue: you get it by courageous acts."

Groundbreaking biochemist and first African American woman to receive a PhD in chemistry in the United States (Columbia, 1947). Her father, a postal clerk whose chemistry studies were cut short by lack of funds, encouraged her love of science. She did seminal research on histones at the Rockefeller Institute, then transferred to Columbia (1955) and Albert Einstein College (1960) to work with Dr. Quentin Demming; their pioneering work examined the relationship between cholesterol, clogged arteries, and heart attacks. Daly recruited minority students, and in retirement established a Queens College scholarship for African American physics and chemistry majors in memory of her father.

Martin Luther King Jr.
(1929–1968)

"Injustice anywhere is a threat to justice everywhere."

American civil rights leader known for activism through nonviolent protest, minister, and winner of the 1964 Nobel Peace Prize. As minister of the Dexter Avenue Baptist Church in Montgomery and a member of the NAACP executive committee, he took on leadership of the 1955 Montgomery bus boycott; he was arrested, his house was bombed, and he emerged as an iconic figure in the intensifying fight for civil rights. Elected president of the Southern Christian Leadership Council in 1957, he drew on Gandhi's nonviolent strategies. From 1960 on he served as co-pastor of his father's Ebenezer Baptist Church in Atlanta, while traveling wherever there was injustice. He wrote five books; spoke more than 2,500 times at protests; organized voter registration drives; was arrested at least twenty times, assaulted at least four times, and featured on the cover of *Time* Magazine.

He conferred with presidents, delivered his famous "I Have a Dream" speech during the 1963 March on Washington, and was the youngest man ever to have won the Nobel Peace Prize. He was assassinated in Memphis in 1968.

Maya Angelou
(1928–2014)

"When people show you who they are, believe them the first time."

Writer, actor, director, producer, and activist. A single mother who grew up in the Jim Crow South, she worked as a fry cook, a calypso dancer, a civil rights coordinator, a foreign correspondent, and a college professor. She was versatile and resilient. She knew how to make fierce beauty out of pain. Her friends included Malcolm X and writer James Baldwin, who said her first autobiography, *I Know Why the Caged Bird Sings* (1970), "liberates the reader into life." Her first book of poetry, *Just Give Me a Cool Drink of Water 'fore I Diiie* (1971), was nominated for a Pulitzer Prize; her performance in the television miniseries *Roots* (1977) earned her an Emmy nomination; and in 1993, she delivered her poem "On the Pulse of the Morning" at the inauguration of Bill Clinton. Barack Obama presented her with the Presidential Medal of Freedom in 2011.

"I've learned that people will forget what you said, people will forget what you did, but people will never forget how you made them feel."

"Prejudice is a burden that confuses the past, threatens the future and renders the present inaccessible."

Michael Jordan
"MJ"
(1963–)

"You must expect great things of yourself before you can do them."

Widely considered the greatest basketball player of all time, he was cut from his high school's varsity team as a 5-foot 11-inch sophomore. He grew to 6 feet 6 inches, and the legendary Celtic Larry Bird called him "God disguised as Michael Jordan." Also known as "Air Jordan" and "His Airness," he spent 13 of his 15 NBA seasons with the Chicago Bulls, winning six NBA championships. A shooting guard for most of his career, he was a prolific scorer, a quick and tough defender (ranking third in NBA history in total steals), and an intense competitor, equally hard on opponents and teammates. In retirement he was the first NBA star to become a billionaire, and his charities include Habitat for Humanity and the Make-a-Wish Foundation. He has given generously to disaster relief efforts and in the wake of George Floyd's killing announced major gifts to organizations dedicated to "ensuring racial equality, social justice and greater access to education."

Miles Davis
(1926–1991)

"Man, sometimes it takes you a long time to sound like yourself."

Innovative trumpet player, bandleader, and composer; called the jazz musician with the most profound influence on rock. His groundbreaking album *Kind of Blue* (1959) is the best-selling jazz recording of all time. The son of an Illinois dental surgeon, he studied classical music at Juilliard but dropped out in 1945 and joined the great Charlie Parker's quintet. From the extroverted exuberance of bebop his music developed into something cooler; it wasn't technical feats other musicians learned from him, but something in his phrasing and sense of space. He overcame a heroin addiction and left behind one style after another, collaborating generously and learning from other musicians as he endlessly reinvented himself and his art. Of his musical phrasing, he said,

"I always listen to what I can leave out."

Misty Copeland
(1982–)

"Belonging shouldn't mean you are like everyone else."

Ballet dancer and first African American female principal dancer of the American Ballet Company, Copeland was a 13-year-old living in a motel room when she discovered ballet. By 14 she was the winner of a national ballet contest. Starting late and developing her gifts with remarkable speed, she overcame injuries and an eating disorder. She hopes to see more diversity on the stage when she's "sixty years old, watching in the audience," and more diversity in the audience, too. She has said,

"You can start late, look different, be uncertain and still succeed."

Muhammad Ali
(1942–2016)

"Float like a butterfly, sting like a bee. His hands can't hit what his eyes can't see."

Born Cassius Marcellus Clay, this heavyweight boxing champion was one of the best boxers of all time. A brilliant showman, he was able to use the media against his opponents in an unparalleled way. Born and raised in Louisville, Kentucky, he won gold in the 1960 Olympics but was embittered when white Louisville restaurant staff refused to serve the "Olympic nigger." He became a professional champion and converted to Islam, leaving his "slave name" behind; he won the world heavyweight title from Sonny Liston in a 1964 upset and successfully defended the title eight times before being stripped of it and suspended from boxing when he resisted the military draft in 1967. ("I ain't got nothing against no Viet Cong; no Viet Cong ever called me nigger," he said.) The Supreme Court granted him conscientious objector status in 1971, but not before he lost what should have been his prime boxing years; to most people's surprise he went on to win again (the Rumble in the Jungle, against George Foreman in 1974) and again (the Thrilla in Manila, against Joe Frazier in 1975) and again before losing his last few bouts and retiring in 1981, already showing symptoms of Parkinson's disease, a condition some attributed to the 200,000 blows he had absorbed in his career, though he denied that. He retired as a three-time heavyweight champion and *Sports Illustrated*'s choice for the greatest athlete of the twentieth century.

Neil deGrasse Tyson
(1958–)

"The good thing about science is that it's true whether or not you believe in it."

Astrophysicist and renowned science communicator and educator. Hooked on astronomy by a visit to the Hayden Planetarium when he was nine, Tyson studied it obsessively in his teens. He earned his PhD from Columbia (1991) and has held positions

at the University of Maryland, Princeton, and the American Museum of Natural History; since 1994 he has directed the Hayden Planetarium, or Great Sphere, with its Star Theater (where "space shows" present scientific visualizations of up-to-date astrophysical findings) above and Big Bang Theater (with a four-minute program on the birth of the universe narrated by Liam Neeson) below. Grateful for the planetarium staff who "invested their time and energy" in him as "a kid," he feels a duty to pass the favor on to new generations and does it with humor and verve. In books, articles, TV and YouTube appearances, and even federal committee assignments, he makes science accessible and routinely shatters stereotypes.

Nelson Mandela
(1918–2013)

"It always seems impossible until it's done."

Nelson Rolihlahla Mandela was an anti-apartheid activist, the first Black president of South Africa, and winner of the 1993 Nobel Peace Prize. In 1948, only whites were allowed to vote in the South African general election, and the winning National Party quickly enacted a system of laws to oppress Black people: apartheid. Mandela, a leader in the opposition African

National Congress (ANC), spent 27 years in jail for resistance activities; released in 1990, he worked with white President F. W. de Klerk to negotiate an end to apartheid. Elected in a multiracial general election in 1994, Mandela headed a coalition government that adopted a new constitution and established a Truth and Reconciliation Commission to address past wrongs. Although he was sometimes controversial and said himself, "I was not a messiah, but an ordinary man who had become a leader because of extraordinary circumstances," Mandela became an icon of democracy, one of the world's most revered men.

"I learned that courage was not the absence of fear, but the triumph over it. The brave man is not he who does not feel afraid, but he who conquers that fear."

"For to be free is not merely to cast off one's chains, but to live in a way that respects and enhances the freedom of others."

Oprah Gail Winfrey
(1954–)

"You get in life what you have the courage to ask for."

Awarding-winning actor and producer, widely believed to be "the most influential woman in the world"; a billionaire who was born in poverty in Mississippi to a teenaged single

mom and survived girlhood challenges in Milwaukee. Sent to live with her biological father in Nashville as a teenager, she became a popular honors student, won a scholarship to Tennessee State, and started in media. Her *Oprah Winfrey Show* (1986–2011) won 47 Daytime Emmy Awards before 2000, when she chose to remove it from contention. Her spontaneous, empathetic style made talk shows more confessional ("Oprahfication," some called it). She has used her influence to boost African American political campaigns and good literature, and her wealth to support philanthropic causes. She has had celebrated roles in *The Color Purple* (1985), *Beloved* (which she produced and starred in in 1998), and other films.

Patricia Hill Collins
(1948–)

"Most activism is brought about by us ordinary people."

Professor and sociologist whose work focuses on race, gender, class, sexuality, and nationality. She first won national notice for her 1990 book *Black Feminist Thought*. Born in Philadelphia, Pennsylvania to working-class parents, she attended Philadelphia High School for Girls during the desegregation process of the 1960s and developed an early interest in sociology, feminism, and activism for civil rights. She majored in sociology at Brandeis (1969) and earned a master's degree in teaching at Harvard (1970); served as a teacher, curriculum specialist, and administrator in the Boston area; married; and completed her Brandeis doctorate (1984). As a professor at the University of Cincinnati and more recently the University of Maryland, she has published many books and articles, exploring questions such as how social structures affect the experience and development of young people.

"Challenging power structures from the inside…requires learning to speak multiple languages of power convincingly."

Paul Robeson
(1898–1976)

"Artists are the gatekeepers of truth. We are civilization's radical voice."

Singer, actor, and civil rights activist, bass baritone Paul Leroy Robeson was a star athlete and valedictorian at Rutgers College and earned his law degree from Columbia University while playing NFL football on weekends. His concerts brought Negro spirituals to a wide audience, and as an actor he shone in lead roles as Eugene O'Neill's Emperor Jones and Shakespeare's Othello. Early in his career he thought African Americans could best fight racism by demonstrating excellence, but in Europe during the 1930s he became convinced that "the artist must take sides. He must elect to fight for freedom or slavery." When World War II broke out, Robeson resumed his film career in the US but objected to demeaning roles. In 1946 he warned President Truman that if lynching was not ended by federal legislation, "the Negroes will defend themselves": Truman ended their meeting, saying the time was not right. Robeson, suspected by the FBI of dangerous left-wing tendencies, was blacklisted during the McCarthy years and lost his passport from 1950 to 1958. His career never fully recovered.

"The answer to injustice is not to silence the critic, but is to end injustice."

Ralph Ellison
(1914–1994)

"I am invisible, understand, simply because people refuse to see me."

Writer whose influential novel, *The Invisible Man*, won the National Book Award in 1953. Growing up in Oklahoma, Ellison worked as a shoeshine boy, a busboy, a waiter, a dentist's assistant. In 1936 he moved from Tuskegee Institute to New York, where Langston Hughes introduced him to left-leaning Black writers and artists. Ellison was drawn to the Communist Party in the 1930s but disillusioned by its failure to support African Americans; like his protagonist in *The Invisible Man*, he was alienated by both Southern and Northern varieties of racism. Yet after living briefly in Rome he returned to the US. He published the essay collection *Shadow and Act* (1964); taught at Bard, Rutgers, and Yale; and worked endlessly on his second novel, *Juneteenth*, which was published after his death.

Rennie Harris
(1964–)

"The work has to have room to breathe."

Born Lorenzo Harris, renowned artistic director, choreographer, and promoter of hip-hop dance. Grew up in North Philadelphia; at about the age of 12, founded his first dance group, Cobra III; and at 15, started teaching hip-hop at the Smithsonian Institution. His Scanner Boys held their last performance at Philadelphia's 30th Street Train Station in 1992, as he created Rennie Harris Puremovement to preserve and disseminate hip-hop culture. With numerous awards and honorary doctorates from Bates College and Columbia College, Harris and his company were chosen as cultural ambassadors by the Obama administration and toured the Middle East. Through teaching and artistic work alike, he communicates and disseminates hip-hop culture.

"If you really look at hip-hop dance, it's really a rite-of-passage thing. You never see the arms release down. They're always up in fighting position. It's going to war. What do we say? We say you're going to battle. You go out there and fight."

Richard Wright
(1908–1960)

"Literature is a struggle over the nature of reality."

Best known for his short story collection *Uncle Tom's Children* (1938), his novel *Native Son* (1940), and his autobiography *Black Boy* (1945), Wright endured a harsh childhood. He spent time in an orphanage and more time in his strict grandparents' home, where beatings happened but books were not allowed. In 1927 he left the Jim Crow South for Chicago, where he worked for the Federal Writers' Project; in 1937 he moved to New York, where he edited leftist periodicals and published militant poems. *Native Son* was a great success, the first Book-of-the-Month-Club selection by an African American writer, yet Wright was dogged by controversy. Some critics objected to his bitter anger against racial injustice. He moved to Paris in 1947, where he wrote novels, nonfiction, and thousands of haiku—poems that linked the seasons of soul and nature, his daughter said, enabling him "to reach out to the black boy part of himself still stranded in a South that continued to live in his dreams."

"Our too-young and too-new America, lusty because it is lonely, aggressive because it is afraid, insists upon seeing the world in terms of good and bad, the holy and the evil, the high and the low, the white and the black; our America is frightened of fact, of history, of processes, of necessity. It hugs the easy way of damning those whom it cannot understand, of excluding those who look different, and it salves its conscience with a self-draped cloak of righteousness."

Robert Johnson
(1911–1938)

"The blues is a low down achin' chill."

Mississippi guitarist, singer, and songwriter, little known in his time but now considered one of the most influential blues musicians in history. Robert Leroy Johnson played on street corners and juke joints, took part in only two low-fidelity recording sessions, and died of disputed causes, one story being that he was poisoned by the jealous husband of a woman with whom

he had flirted. Three different churchyards claim to be his resting place, and legend holds that he sold his soul to the devil at a crossroad to gain musical genius. Decades after his death, Columbia Records reissued some of his work as *King of the Delta Blues*, influencing Eric Clapton, Bob Dylan, Keith Richards, and other rising stars. Johnson's work includes "Crossroads," "Love in Vain," "Stop Breaking Down," and "Terraplane Blues."

Ronald K. Brown
(1957–)

"I don't come with preconceived ideas."

Dancer and choreographer; founded the Evidence Dance Company in 1985 with a mission "to promote understanding of the human experience in the African Diaspora." Choreographing not only for Evidence but also for the Alvin Ailey American Dance Company, the Jacob's Pillow Dance Festival, and others, Brown has worked with and influenced leading figures in modern dance—even as he draws inspiration from African and Caribbean traditions and from historic experiences as painful and constricting as the Middle Passage. Deeply spiritual, his dance gives evidence of things unseen, of suffering and endurance and triumph.

Ronald McNair
(1950–1986)

"Whether or not you reach your goals in life depends entirely on how well you prepare for them and how badly you want them."

NASA astronaut, physicist, black belt karate instructor, and jazz saxophonist. Flew as a mission specialist aboard the shuttle *Challenger* in February 1984, the second African American in space. As a boy, he harvested cotton and tobacco in South Carolina and ran into trouble with the law at the age of nine when a librarian called police and his mother because he was trying to check out books from the whites-only library. He went on to earn his PhD from MIT in 1976 and was awarded three honorary doctorates. He advocated better state funding for poor and minority schools, and took every opportunity to tell young students, "You're better than good enough. . . . If you're willing to work hard, sacrifice, and struggle, then I proclaim today that you're better than good enough." He worked hard even at his hobbies, studying the physics of martial arts and endlessly practicing the original saxophone solo he planned to play on the 1986 *Challenger* mission. After the mission, he planned to return to South Carolina, to make it clear that Blacks who

left and prospered could go home and give back. He died when the *Challenger* exploded nine miles over the Atlantic. Schools, scholarships, and a crater on the moon have been named for him, and in 2011 his hometown library was renamed "The Ronald McNair Life History Center."

"True courage comes in enduring... persevering...and believing in oneself."

Rosa Parks
(1913–2005)

"I have learned over the years that when one's mind is made up, this diminishes fear; knowing what must be done does away with fear."

Civil rights activist whose refusal to give up her seat to a white passenger on December 1, 1955, led to a year-long boycott of buses in Montgomery, Alabama. Rosa Louise McCauley Parks was hurrying home from work to send out notices for an NAACP election and prepare a teen workshop she was running, "So it was not a time for me to be planning to be arrested," she said, but she was tired of being humiliated. People respected her; Martin Luther King Jr. called her "one of the finest citizens of Montgomery." Her arrest triggered an attack on Jim Crow laws. The call for a bus boycott went out from pulpits on December 4;

the Women's Political Council distributed 35,000 flyers; the *Montgomery Advertiser* ran a front-page article; and if they couldn't take cabs or carpool, Black citizens walked—some more than 20 miles a day— to avoid taking a bus. In November 1956 the Supreme Court outlawed segregation on buses. The court order reached Montgomery on December 20, 1956, and the boycott ended the next day. Violence against civil rights leaders did not. The arrest of Rosa Parks was one iconic moment in the long struggle for civil rights.

"People always say that I didn't give up my seat because I was tired, but that isn't true. I was not tired physically.... No, the only tired I was, was tired of giving in."

Roy Ottoway Wilkins
(1901–1981)

"Muffle your rage. Get smart instead of muscular."

Civil rights activist and executive director of the National Association for the Advancement of Colored People. With a University of Minnesota degree in sociology, St. Louis native Wilkins edited African American newspapers (*The Appeal; The Call*) before going to work for the NAACP as assistant secretary in 1931. In 1934 he became editor of *The Crisis*, the NAACP's official magazine. In

1950, with leaders of the Brotherhood of Sleeping Car Porters and the National Jewish Community Relations Advisory Council, he founded the Leadership Council on Civil Rights, a coalition whose strategic efforts brought about landmark legislation. He headed the NAACP from 1955 until his retirement in 1977 and helped lead the 1963 March on Washington. While sometimes criticized for his moderate approach, he earned the respectful nickname "Mr. Civil Rights," testifying patiently before numerous Congressional hearings.

Satchel Paige
(1906–1982)

"I ain't ever had a job, I just always played baseball."

Leroy Robert Paige was a professional baseball player and the first former Negro League Baseball player inducted into the National Baseball Hall of Fame. The right-hander learned to pitch in reform school (so the school wasn't a waste, he said) and kept doing it through the Depression and World War II, winning for teams from Kansas City ("You'd look at that big ol' slow arm movin' and—*chooo*—that ball's just right by you," an opposing batter recalled) to Puerto Rico. ("It took special eyes to see his pitches," a pitcher there said.)

Hall of Fame pitcher Dizzy Dean called him "the pitcher with the greatest stuff I ever saw." Joe DiMaggio called him "the best I've ever faced, and the fastest." Ted Williams said he was "the greatest pitcher in baseball." After a crippling arm injury in 1938, he made his way back into the game, supplementing his legendary fastballs with an amazing repertoire of slower pitches that deceived batters. In 1948 the Cleveland Indians signed him as the first African American pitcher in the American League, and at 42 the oldest Major League rookie ever. He kept playing well into his fifties, jangling around gently as he moved and not looking back to see what might be gaining on him.

"Age is a case of mind over matter. If you don't mind, it don't matter."

"The only change is that baseball turned Paige from a second-class citizen to a second-class immortal."

Serena Williams
(1981–)

"You have to believe in yourself when no one else does."

Serena Jameka Williams has been a professional tennis player since 1995; ranked #1 in singles by the Women's Tennis Association eight times between 2002 and 2017; and winner of 23 Grand Slam singles titles—a record for

the Open Era, in which professionals are allowed to compete with amateurs. In the Williams Era, two Black sisters—Venus and Serena, coached by their father—have inspired generations of Black and multiracial girls to compete. Serena, famous for recovering from injuries and setbacks, returned from pregnancy in 2020 to win the ASB Classic, becoming the first woman in the Open Era to win titles in four different decades—the 1990s, the 2000s, the 2010s, and the 2020s. The Williams sisters are also famous for supporting charitable causes from education and health to the Equal Justice Initiative.

Shirley Chisholm
(1924–2005)

"If they don't give you a seat at the table, bring a folding chair."

First African American woman elected to Congress and first to run for president of the United States. Born in Brooklyn, New York, to immigrants from the Caribbean, Shirley Anita St. Hill spent part of her childhood (1929–1934) with her grandmother, absorbing a sense of dignity and a West Indian accent. Politically active in Brooklyn College (where she won prizes for debate), she married Conrad Chisholm in 1949, earned her MA in 1952, worked in early education through 1964, and in 1953 plunged into ward politics. "Unbought and unbossed," as she told her constituents, she served in the New York State Assembly (1965–1968) and the US House of Representatives (1968–1983). Her 1972 presidential campaign was underfunded, but she used the platform to advocate racial and gender equality, an end to the Vietnam War, and compassionate treatment of all who are in need.

"I want to be remembered as a woman ... who dared to be a catalyst of change."

Sidney Poitier
(1927–)

"I am the me I choose to be."

Actor, director, and movie producer. The son of Bahamian tomato farmers, born prematurely while they were visiting Miami, he grew up on the farm and moved to the US at 15. He washed dishes in New York restaurants, improved his reading skills, worked to lose his accent, and by the 1950s was building a career in the movies. In 1967, as the civil rights movement seemed poised for success, he played the leading men in three remarkable films: the idealistic teacher who won over white teenagers in *To Sir, with Love*; the physician whose engagement to their daughter shocked white liberal parents in *Guess Who's Coming to Dinner*; and the ace

homicide detective outthinking skeptical white policemen in *In the Heat of the Night*. "There's a mythological aspect to Poitier," said a critic. Uneasy about the idealized roles he was offered, he still saw value in portraying civil characters who broke the stereotypes. His many awards include Golden Globe and Academy Best Actor awards for *Lilies of the Field* (1963) and a Presidential Medal of Freedom (2009).

"You're gonna have to be twice as good as the white folks in order to get half as much."

Simone Biles
(1997–)

"I'd rather regret the risks that didn't work out than the chances I didn't take at all."

The most decorated American gymnast in history. Born in Columbus, Ohio, and raised by her grandparents in Spring, Texas, Biles first tried gymnastics on a day-care field trip when she was six; she began training with coach Aimee Boorman at eight, and by 2011 she was competing in elite contests. Homeschooling allowed time for rigorous training, and despite injuries and other setbacks, in 2013 she became the first African American to win the all-around title at the World Artistic Gymnastics. She won four gold medals at the 2016 Summer Olympics in Rio de Janeiro. In 2018 she confirmed

that she was a victim of Larry Nassar, the former USA gymnastics physician sentenced for abuse—but she went on to perform more difficult routines on vault (2018) and in floor exercise (2019) than ever before seen in the women's sport, including two unique skills that are named after her, the Biles and the Biles II. Her 30 Olympic and World Championship medals are the most ever won by an American gymnast and the third most in the world history of the sport.

Sojourner Truth
(1797?–1883)

"I am pleading that my people may have their rights restored, for they have long been toiling, and yet had no reward."

Abolitionist, speaker, and women's rights advocate, Isabella "Belle" Baumfree was born into slavery in Dutch-speaking Swartekill, New York. In 1806 she was auctioned off with a flock of sheep for $100; her new master beat her daily, once with a bundle of rods, for such faults as not speaking English. In 1826, the year before New York emancipated its enslaved people, she escaped with an infant daughter to an abolitionist family in New Paltz. When her former owner illegally sold her five-year-old son in Alabama, she sued him and recovered the child, becoming one of the first Black women

to win a court case against a white man. She became deeply religious and in 1843, telling friends, "The Spirit calls me, and I must go," she took the name Sojourner Truth and began traveling and preaching the abolitionist cause. She was a powerful speaker and singer, able to quiet a mob. She reached listeners in person and readers through an autobiography dictated to Olive Gilbert. She was a strong advocate for the rights of Black people and of women before, during, and after the Civil War.

"If women want rights more than they got, why don't they just take them, and not be talking about it."

Spike Lee
(1957–)

"Power is knowing your past."

Film director, producer, screenwriter, actor, and professor, Shelton Jackson "Spike" Lee deserves more awards than he's won. From his groundbreaking *She's Gotta Have It* (1986) on, he has shown complex people of color—often upscale and sophisticated, and always in circumstances that challenge them on multiple levels. *Do the Right Thing* (1989) has been called one of the ten greatest films of the 1980s or of all time. The characters in his feature films clash and disagree; the effect may be richly comic, but also calls on audiences to respond with nuanced understanding. His compassionate documentaries probe hard topics: the life of Malcolm X, the Birmingham church bombing, the aftermath of Hurricane Katrina, and a Black policeman's infiltration of the Ku Klux Klan. In 2015, Lee received his first Oscar, not for acting, directing, or Best Picture, but for himself: an Academy Honorary Award as "a champion of independent film and an inspiration to young filmmakers."

"But I think that patriotism is when you speak truth to power. It's patriotic to speak out about the injustices in this country. That is being an American patriot."

Stephanie Wilson
(1966–)

"The sky, or outer space, really is the limit for [young girls'] aspirations."

American engineer and NASA astronaut, veteran of three space flights. Born in Boston and raised in Pittsfield, Massachusetts. Wilson's father encouraged her to follow him into engineering; a middle-school interview with an astronomer deepened her interest in space. She earned her BS in engineering from Harvard (1988) and her MS in aerospace engineering from the University of Texas (1992), began work

for the Jet Propulsion Laboratory in Pasadena after graduate school, and was selected for NASA's Astronaut Training Program in 1996. Wilson has flown three shuttle missions, and on October 18, 2019, she was the Houston ground controller for the first all-woman spacewalk.

Stevie Wonder
(1950–)

"Just because a man lacks the use of his eyes doesn't mean he lacks vision."

Singer, songwriter, musician, and record producer; winner of 25 Grammys and numerous other awards for both music and civil rights work. Stevland Hardaway Judkins was blind at his premature birth in Saginaw, Michigan. His songwriter mother raised him in Detroit, where he played piano, harmonica, and drums; sang with a friend on street corners and at occasional parties; and wrote "Lonely Boy," a song that landed him a Motown contract at the age of 11. As Little Stevie Wonder he had great success, and at 13 he was the youngest artist ever to top the Billboard Hot 100 with his single "Fingertips." His voice changed; he dropped the "Little" from his stage name and grew to maturity as one of the most influential Black artists of the early 1970s. By age 26 his hits included "Fingertips, Part 2," "My Cherie Amour," "Signed, Sealed and Delivered I'm

Yours," "Superstition," "Superwoman (Where Were You When I Needed You)," "You Are the Sunshine of My Life," "Living for the City," and "Isn't She Lovely?" (1976, for his newborn daughter), and he had produced three successive Grammy Award–winning albums: *Innervisions* (1974), *Fulfillingness' First Finale* (1975), and *Songs in the Key of Life* (1976). The best-selling of his many songs is "I Just Called to Say I Love You" (1984). He has sold more than 100 million records and is known for his generosity to philanthropic and civil rights causes. He received the Presidential Medal of Freedom from Barack Obama in 2014.

Ta-Nehisi Coates
(1975–)

"But race is the child of racism, not the father."

Author and journalist whose book *Between the World and Me*, written as a letter to his teenaged son, won the 2015 National Book Award for Nonfiction. He grew up in Baltimore, surrounded by books and family. His librarian father, a former Black Panther, founded and ran Black Classic Press; his teacher mother made Ta-Nehisi write essays when he misbehaved. His college career was disrupted when police shot friend Prince Jones in a case of mistaken identity—a trauma that helps inform *Between the World and Me*. Coates

wrote for various publications before settling for a decade at *The Atlantic*, where he became a senior editor. Major features from the Obama years, including "Fear of a Black President" and "The Case for Reparations," are reprinted in his second book, *We Were Eight Years in Power: An American Tragedy* (2017). Having left *The Atlantic* in 2018, Coates published his first novel, *The Water Dancer*, in 2019; he also writes the *Black Panther* series for Marvel Comics. His many awards include a 2015 Genius Grant from the MacArthur Foundation.

Thurgood Marshall
(1908–1993)

"Where you see wrong or inequality or injustice, speak out because this is your country. This is your democracy. Make it. Protect it. Pass it on."

The first African American justice on the Supreme Court of the United States (1967–1991), Marshall rose to national prominence as a lawyer for the National Association for the Advancement of Colored People (1934–1961), where from 1940 on he was the founding director of the Legal Defense Fund. He argued 32 cases before the Supreme Court and won 29 of them, including Brown v. Board of Education (1954), which held that racial segregation in public education violates the Equal Protection Clause of the Fourteenth Amendment. He knew the Constitution well—as a schoolboy "hellraiser" he was routinely assigned passages to memorize for punishment—and he learned to argue from his father, a railroad porter who took him to watch court cases and debated them afterward. At Howard Law School he was inspired to use the law as a weapon against institutional racism by Dean Charles Hamilton Houston, who pushed students to be "social engineers rather than lawyers." Marshall won cases against whites-only primaries in Texas, restrictive covenants that kept Blacks from buying or renting homes, and other mechanisms for enforcing inequality. In 1961, President Kennedy appointed him to the Second Circuit Court of Appeals, and six years later President Johnson nominated him to the Supreme Court, where as a judge he was first part of a liberal majority and later a powerful dissenter. He celebrated "the Constitution as a living document, including the Bill of Rights and other amendments protecting individual freedoms and human rights"—it was those rights and freedoms that mattered more than the words he'd once memorized.

Tommie Smith
(1944–)

"We had to be seen because we couldn't be heard."

Olympic track-and-field gold medalist who raised a black gloved fist on the podium at the 1968 summer Olympics with teammate John Carlos in protest of civil rights injustices. It was an iconic moment. The gloved fist represented power; the bowed head, prayer; and the shoeless feet, Black poverty. Smith and Carlos were influenced by the Olympic Project for Human Rights, which called for boycotting the games unless white-ruled South Africa and Rhodesia were uninvited; Muhammed Ali's world heavyweight boxing title was restored; Avery Brundage—who in 1936 had worked against a US boycott of the games in Hitler's Munich—stepped down as President of the International Olympic Committee; and more African Americans were hired as assistant coaches. Expelled from the games for their gesture, Smith and Carlos faced a period of ostracism, death threats, and even homelessness before finally recovering economically. On November 1, 2019, the two were inducted into the Olympic and Paralympic Hall of Fame; their citation says they courageously stood up for racial equality.

Toni Morrison
(1931–2019)

"The search for love and identity runs through most everything I write."

First African American and first Black woman of any nationality to receive the Nobel Prize for literature, in 1996. Morrison's eleven novels include *The Bluest Eye* (1970), *Sula* (1973), *Song of Solomon* (1977), *Beloved* (1987), *Jazz* (1992), *Paradise* (1998), and *God Help the Child* (2015); she also published two plays, a libretto, nonfiction, short stories, and with her younger son, Slade Morrison, seven children's books. She was born and raised in Lorain, Ohio, an integrated town where she absorbed African American folklore from her parents and novelistic skills from favorite authors such as Jane Austen and Leo Tolstoy. She graduated from Howard University, earned a master's degree from Cornell, married Jamaican architect Harold Morrison in 1958, and began a career in editing after their 1964 divorce. As the first Black woman with a senior position in the Random House fiction department, she contributed to the growth of Black literature, editing a generation of poets, radicals, and novelists. In 1983 she left publishing to spend more time on writing, and from 1989 to 2006 she was a professor at Princeton University.

Along with critical acclaim (her numerous awards included a National Book Critics Circle Award for *Song of Solomon*, a Pulitzer Prize for *Beloved*, and a 2012 Presidential Medal of Freedom), her writing met with commercial success; Oprah Winfrey, who starred in the movie version of *Beloved*, said, "there would have been no Oprah's Book Club if this woman had not chosen to share her love of words with the world." Morrison said she had to write; it was the way she understood the world.

"I'm interested in how men are educated, how women relate to each other, how we are able to love, how we balance political and personal forces, who survives in certain situations and who doesn't and, specifically, how these and other universal issues relate to African Americans."

Tupac Shakur
"2Pac"
(1971–1996)

"Death is not the greatest loss in life. The greatest loss is what dies inside while still alive. Never surrender."

Rap star whose lyrics gave voice to marginalized communities but who was also criticized for a violent lifestyle and for rap lyrics that glorified violence. Born in East Harlem of parents active in the Black Panther Party, he was named after Tupac Amaru II, descendent of the last Incan ruler, who was executed in Peru after revolting against Spanish rule; "I wanted him to know he was part of a world culture and not just from a neighborhood," his mother explained. In high school in Baltimore, he acted in Shakespearean plays, danced in the *Nutcracker* ballet, and connected with a Communist youth group. After moving to the West Coast in 1988, he began recording in 1989 and rose to stardom after his 1991 debut album *2Pacalypse Now*. He appeared in films, confronted police, spent time in jail, and rapped about the glamor and despair of a gangster lifestyle. "All we know is violence," he sang in "Trapped," but he told an interviewer to let children know "because I'm talking about it doesn't mean it's OK." His last studio album, *The 7 Day Theory*, released after his death, was certified 4x Platinum. Killed in a drive-by shooting, Tupac was elected to the Rock and Roll Hall of Fame in his first year of eligibility.

W.E.B Du Bois
(1868–1963)

"*One ever feels his 'twoness' — an American, a Negro; two souls, two thoughts, two unreconciled strivings; two warring ideals in one dark body, whose dogged strength alone keeps it from being torn asunder.*"

Public intellectual, civil rights activist, author, and cofounder of the National Association for the Advancement of Colored People in 1909, William Edward Burghardt Du Bois was born and raised in Great Barrington, Massachusetts. He was intellectually gifted, completing bachelor's degrees from Fisk (1888) and Harvard (1890), studying at the University of Berlin, and becoming the first African American to earn a Harvard PhD (1895). He became a sociology professor at Atlanta University, where he taught brilliantly, published ground-breaking scholarly works, and engaged in civil rights activism. He published his seminal book *The Souls of Black Folk* in 1903. He saw little point to art that didn't work as propaganda or scholarship that didn't advance humanity. There was exploitation in colonized Africa and Asia and racist violence in the United States, and for rampant injustice "the cure wasn't simply telling people the truth, it was inducing them to act on the truth." He fought for quality Black education and against lynching. Seeing capitalism as a cause of racism, he was open to socialist ideas, prompting the FBI to investigate him for possible subversive activity. In 1950, for his role in publicizing the Stockholm Peace Initiative, he was accused of acting as the agent of a foreign power and his passport

was revoked for eight years. In 1961 he went to Ghana to work on an encyclopedia of the African diaspora, and the US again refused to renew his passport, so he became a citizen of Ghana and died there at the age of 95, the day before Martin Luther King delivered his "I Have a Dream" speech on the steps of the Lincoln Memorial in Washington, DC.

Zora Neal Hurston
(1891–1960)

"*Love makes your soul crawl out from its hiding place.*"

Most famous for *Their Eyes Were Watching God* (1937), Hurston wrote other novels, plays, essays, an autobiography titled *Dust Tracks on a Road* (1942), and short stories—one of them called "Spunk." She grew up in Eatonville, Florida, graduated from Barnard College in 1928, and did graduate work at Columbia. A Southern folklorist and anthropologist, a political conservative, friend of the Harlem Renaissance, and fighter for justice, she worked as a journalist or even a maid when she had to, believed in facing reality, and died poor. Near her unmarked grave, novelist Alice Walker set a memorial that said simply: A GENIUS OF THE SOUTH.

Photo by Dorothe Nanji

Shani Mahiri King
is a law professor at the University
of Florida, where he is director
of the Center on Children and
Families and an Associate Director
of the Center on Race and Race
Relations. Shani is the father
of a nine-year-old daughter and
a six-year-old son, for whom he
wrote the picture book *Have I Ever
Told You?* (Tilbury House, 2019).

Photo by Justin Bettman

Bobby C. Martin Jr. is co-founder
of Champions Design, a branding
and design agency in New York
City, and faculty member
of the graduate design program
at the School of Visual Arts,
where he earned an MFA in 2003.
Bobby's design credits include
the June 24, 2020 *New York
Times* Sunday Magazine cover
"What Is Owed" and the April 2018
special edition of *The Atlantic*
magazine honoring Martin Luther
King Jr. Bobby's son was born
in 2019 and inspired him
to take on this project.

Text © 2021 by Shani Mahiri King
Illustrations and Design © 2021 by Champions Design

Hardcover ISBN 978-0-88448-889-7

Tilbury House Publishers
Thomaston, Maine
www.tilburyhouse.com

Library of Congress Control Number: 2020947553

Printed in the United States of America

10 9 8 7 6 5 4 3 2 1

ISPOS ATTUCKS C.T. VIVIAN A. STOKELY CARMICHAEL HUEYN
ANGSTON HUJAMES BALDWIN RALPHELLISON MAYA ANGELOU TO
EX HALEY UGHES GWENDOLYN BROOKS ALICEWALKER AUDR
LSMITH PHILLIS WHEATLEY PUBLIC EN ERIC GARNER REKIA
MIHENDRIXOTNOTORIOUS B.I.G. JACQUELINEMY COUNTEE CULLEN B
EDERICK DOUGLASS WEST STEVIE LOUIS ARMSTRONG NIKKI GIOVA
UINCY COUNT GLASS BEYONCÉ WONDERSTRONG MARIAN ANDER
JONES BASIE COLEMAN HAWKINSHANI MAHIRI KING JAY-
HUCK BERRY JOHN COLTRANE ROBERT BATTLE BOB MARLEY HERBI
COOLJ FRED DIE GRAY WALTER SCOTT SROY ELDRIDGE CHARLIE PA
CHAEL DEAN MUHAMMAD ALI MICHAEL TAMIR RICE GWEN IFILL CH
SON DAVIS SIMONE BILES LISA LESLIE JORDAN ARTHUR ASHE TOM
ORENCE GRIFFITH JOYNER WILLIE SERENA WILLIAMS ALTH
BE BRYANT LEBRON JAMES SANDRA MAYS COLIN KAEPERNICK SU
AIN LOCKE PHILANDO CASTILE BLAND ALEXANDER CRUMMEL
NSTANCE BAKER MOTLEY THURGOODMARSHALL ANNETTE GORDON-REED
EAN-MICHEL BASQUIAT JACOB LAWRENCE MARY FRANCES BE
HLEY BRYAN FAITH RINGGOLD SHERRILYN IFILL KWAME
EIL DEGRASSE KATHERINE JOHNSON JERRY PINKNEY BOBBY C. MART
W TYSON DOROTHY JOHNSON MARIE MAYNARD ERNEST
NG JESSE ERNEST WILKINS VAUGHAN DALY MARGARET JAMES
JR. MARK E. DEAN JEWEL PLUM
YANNA PRESSLEY JOHN BARACK RALPH BUNCHE CAROL MOSELEY BRAU
ARBARA JORDAN COLIN LEW CK OBAMA AUGUST WILSON JOY REID EU
RAH WINFREY MORGAN IS MICHELLE OBAMA ILHAN OMAR DENZ
ROTHY DANDRIDGE POWELL MAXINE WATERS SUSAN RICE MA
JOURNER TRUTH JAMES FREEMAN HARRIET TUBMAN ARTHUR MITCH
EORGE FLOYD RON MES EARL JONES RAYSHARD BROOKS